Photographic Memory:

9 Most Powerful Steps to Remember Anything in Your Life Forever! Reduce Memory Loss, Create Habits to Help You Improve Memory Efficiency, Focus and Clarity! Best to Listen in Car!

© **Copyright 2019 by Tony Bennis - All rights reserved.**

The content contained within this book may not be reproduced, duplicated or transmitted without direct written permission from the author or the publisher.

Under no circumstances will any blame or legal responsibility be held against the publisher, or author, for any damages, reparation, or monetary loss due to the information contained within this book. Either directly or indirectly.

Legal Notice:

This book is copyright protected. This book is only for personal use. You cannot amend, distribute, sell, use, quote or paraphrase any part, or the content within this book, without the consent of the author or publisher.

Disclaimer Notice:

Please note the information contained within this document is for educational and entertainment purposes only. All effort has been executed to present accurate, up to date, and reliable, complete information. No warranties of any kind are declared or implied. Readers acknowledge that the author is not engaging in the rendering of legal, financial, medical or professional advice. The content within this book has been derived from various sources. Please consult a licensed professional before attempting any techniques outlined in this book.

By reading this document, the reader agrees that under no circumstances is the author responsible for any losses, direct or indirect, which are incurred as a result of the use of information contained within this document, including, but not limited to, — errors, omissions, or inaccuracies.

Table of Contents

Introduction....................10

Step 1: Training Your General Memory....................12

    Create a Visual Memory
        Case Study

    Techniques Used for General Memory: Word Association

    Making Information Meaningful
        Example

    Create a Memory Palace

    Remember Using Pictures

    Conclusion

Step 2: Use the Military Method....................22
        Disclaimer

    Steps to Enact the Military Method

    Using the Military Method to Help with Memory-- Practical Example: Ron White, Two-Time USA Memory Champion

    1. "The more you sweat in times of peace, the less you bleed in times of war."

    2. Develop a Positive Mindset: Winning Frame of Mind

    3. Set Small Goals for Your Memorization

    4. Always Face the Consequence of Not Hitting a Goal

    5. Train Your Memory Every Day, Even When You Don't Feel Like It

    Conclusion

Step 3: Improving Your Photographic Memory Diet......................31

How is Memory Connected to Diet?

A Heart-Healthy Diet Can be a Brain-Healthy Diet

The Foods and Drinks that We Recommend You Try for a Better Memory
- Coffee
- Turmeric
- Broccoli
- Dark Chocolate
- Oranges
- Eggs
- Green Tea

Try Diets that Include More Fat and Less Carbs

Intermittent Fasting

Moderate Drinking, So You Can Remember More
- Case Study

Conclusion

Step 4: Sleeping for Memory's Sake.....................41

Why Good Sleep is Important

The Theories Behind Sleep

What Does Sleep Do for Memory?

Example of Korea: Cramming Schools, Rote Memorization, and the Absence of Sleep

Sleep Deprivation Has Dire Consequences for Our Memory

How to Up Your Memory and Enable You To Remember: Sleep!
- Case Study

Conclusion

Step 5: Use Mnemonic Devices to Remember Almost Anything....................51

    The Method of Loci

    Acronyms

    Creating a Memory Class (For Teachers)

    In Different Cultures: Use English names

    Rhymes

    How Do You Memorize that Lengthy Poem? Make an Image of It in Your Mind
        Case Study

    How to Memorize Lines for the Next Town Play
        Case Study: Jemima

    Chunking and Organization
        Case Study: Jason

    Do a Jingle or a Dance to Remember Things Well
        Case Study

    Conclusion

Step 6: Everyday Techniques: Use the Senses....................64

    How to Make Things Real: Create Absurd Images to Remember
        Case Study

    Turn the Sounds of Names that We Learn into Images
        Case Study

    Use as Many of Your Senses As Possible

    When It Comes to Numbers, Use the Same Method
        Case Study

    Use Your Sensory Memory to Re-Create Experiences
        Case Study

Why Sensory Memory Works

How to Use Your Sensory Memory

Why This Technique is For Actors and Everyone
Case Study

Conclusion

Step 7: Use Techniques that Increase Cognitive Activity and Add to Your Memory.....................76

1. **Physical Activity: Working Out**
Case Study

2. **Be Open to New Experiences**
Case Study

3. **Utilize Your Artistic and Creative Skills**
Case Study

4. **Social Connections**
Case Study: Frank

5. **Mindfulness and Meditation**
Case Study

6. **Decrease Anxiety and Stress**
Case Study

7. **Listen to Classical Music or Play an Instrument**
Case Study

Conclusion

Step 8: Take Steps to Increase Mental Alertness....................94

1. **Hydration**
Case Study

2. **Watch the Caffeine**
Case Study

3. Lose the GPS and Find Other Ways to Get Home
   Case Study

4. Pursue a Hobby
   Case Study

Step 9: Study Skills: What You Can Work On Now to Increase Your Photographic Memory....................103

1. Spaced Repetition
   Case Study

2. Use Your Smartphone Apps Including Study Blue and Memrise
   Case Study

3. For Language Classes, Take Vocab Tests Online for Self-Study
   Case Study

4. Draw Images of Stories and The Concepts that You are Studying
   Case Study

5. Recite a Text for Poetry Slams and Other Competitions

6. Use a Memory Peg to Remember Things By What They Rhyme With

7. Slow Down the Studying
   Case Study

8. Watch a documentary on the topic that you're studying.

9. Take Study Breaks
   Case Study: Tracy

10. Find New Study Spaces
    Case Study

11. Never Pull An All-Nighter. Ever.

Case Study
Conclusion......................118

Introduction

How good is your memory? Are you able to remember minute details, or do you forget the names and faces of people that you immediately meet? Many people don't have a good memory and are unable to recall basic information after just glancing at something for a minute. Many of us wish we had a better memory, but we don't know where to start. We are so frustrated with what we cannot remember, even though we try so hard to recall the basic things in our lives. That's one of the reasons we have photos, to capture moments in our lives and memorialize the experiences that we have.

One of the things that people desire is a photographic memory, which is a memory that is able to recall things with vivid accuracy because when you try to remember something, you're able to associate it with an image in your mind automatically. This is the way that we think, and it is the way we can remember things. Our memories are formed by images in our minds to make it easier to recall them. We cannot forget events, people, places, numbers, etc., when we have encoded them into our minds using images that help us to produce a memory of them upon command. Having a photographic memory is an essential step in helping a person remember all the different details of their lives better. And it does not require you to be a genius. All you need is a bit of training and discipline, and you can also refine your memory to have a photographic memory.

This book is going to explain the process of developing your skills to have a photographic memory using different methods and hacks that will help you to make your memory sharper than ever. Although you might think that it requires a lot of talent and innate gifting, we will show you how this is not the case. Instead, our memories are complex repositories of knowledge and information that develop over time and continue expanding and growing, while removing some memories. Our brains are always developing new memories that we can take with us for the rest of our lives. Some remain in our permanent memory, while others are only in our minds for a short period and then are jettisoned with the wind.

As you read through this book, you will discover nine ways that you can make your memory sharper and more photographic than ever. This book begins by introducing you to memory training plans that will significantly help your memory and also a military method that is proven to boost your recall of textual information. Then, we will explain how factors such as sleep, diet, exercise, caffeine, and other things affect your memory's development and its overall well-being. These factors must be considered as you are developing a wellness program, which will enhance your memory.

We thank you for coming with us on this journey into imagination and memory. We hope that you will experience some new insights into how to remember things better and will benefit from each step of the way. Our nine steps are guaranteed to give you the best photographic memory to remember virtually anything you can name. Let's discover the secrets of having this unique and amazing skill together.

Step 1: Training Your General Memory

Everyone wants to have a good memory, but too many of us struggle to have basic memorization skills. The truth is, the world in which we live thrives on ways that does not make us use our memories. We rely on communication and the Internet to store the information in the Cloud, in different documents, and in other storage devices that are within our click and grasp but are not immediately available to us in our minds.

We spend a good deal of our time using electronic devices that store massive amounts of information, which we rely upon every day. We could not think of functioning without Internet or mobile technology, because everything in our life depends on the proper usage of those devices. As a result, we spend very little of our time training our memory to remember basic things. Some people are unable to remember basic numbers such as phone numbers or passwords. The digital age has made us into people who rely less on memory and more on the computers and devices that we use every day to store our memories.

But we are in constant need to remember moments and things, and yet, we always seem to forget the essential elements in our lives. The devices that we use everyday cannot completely store our memories permanently. These devices will eventually fail and will not be able to do all the things that we want them to do. What's more, we could lose these devices, or they could permanently fail and break so that we would not be able to recover the information stored on them.

This brings us to the point of needing to store our memories in our minds. The human brain is one of the most complex and fascinating devices on the planet. We have the power to be hundreds of computers within our brains. Our minds are vacant spaces that store vasts amount of information. By forgetting certain things, we can remember new things.

Create a Visual Memory

One of the essential ways that we can train our memories to visualize what we can do is by recalling through visual and spatial cues. You could try rote memorization of different things without any contextualization. Rote memorization is the consistent act of repetition of something in your mind to remember it better. You may be able to remember those things for a few seconds, minutes, or hours. But after taking a test, you won't be able to remember any of what you had studied or looked at before. This is the case for many people living in Asia, where rote memorization is a crucial educational concept that millions of people are doing every day to promote vocabulary acquisition. However, educational professionals are actively against this approach and think that this does more harm than good by only relying upon short-term memory, which can, indeed, retain vasts amount of information. But what we want to attain is a memory that is long-term, and that retains a lot of information that we can have for a long time. That is where we have to train our general memory.

Case Study

Joshua Foer gave a TED Talk in 2012, where he talked about his experience with memory training, as he participated in a memory competition (Foer, 2012). He started as a journalist, interviewing different participants, and seeing how they did on the competition. However, he wanted to really get inside of the minds of these participants. His study on memory was not too exciting, and he wanted to take his investigation on a deeper level. Moreover, he decided to have a go at doing a memory competition in which he could train his audiovisual memory to remember whatever it was that came to his memory.

In his interviews, Foer talked to different men and women, who were participating in this competition. They were memorizing phone numbers, names of people and faces, among other bits of rote information. As he talked to the participants, he recognized that they also had average memories. They did not have any specialized knowledge or ability. The training of the mind does not have to involve any innate talent for memory. These people, with an average memory, were able to train themselves to remember lots of information within a short period, and they demonstrated an ability that was acquired by studying a method developed by the Ancient Greeks 2,500 years ago, which I will talk about in the following paragraphs.

A long time ago, during the time of the Ancient Greeks, people relied on their memory and cultivated long-term memories. They did this without any reference to other things. Think about the Greek poets, who memorized stories and then recited them out loud. Much of the information and knowledge was imparted to people using the oral tradition, which was a way of training people to remember things they read, places they went to, and other things. Foer gives the example of Simonides, who was a poet, and who recited a long and epic poem to a group of people at a gathering. Unfortunately, during the gathering, there was a disaster that took place, and the building collapsed, in which everyone died, except for the poet, Simonides. Different body parts were scattered across the room, belonging to the people who were there. As he relied on his audiovisual memory, Simonides could remember where each person had sat in the room. For the people who were grieving the loss of their loved ones, Simonides could direct them to the area in the room where their loved ones had been. This is a fantastic testimony of memory and how it can work in someone's favor. Simonides used his visual and spatial memory to recall the locations of where the people were in the room.

This ancient method is one that was used in the competition with different memory champions. Foer talked about how the competitors were put under an MRI scan, and their brains were compared to the average person in the world. The study found that these individuals do not have brains that are that much different from the rest of us. However, there was one crucial difference that he noted. They relied more on spatial and navigational skills within their brains, which allowed them to remember more details.

Techniques Used for General Memory: Word Association

Foer demonstrated different methods to help with memory. One of the most critical memory training techniques is word association, which is basic but important to developing a visual and spatial memory. For example, give a person a name to memorize and see which person can do a better job. Say, you have the name: Baker, and you are given the task of memorizing that name. Or, you are told to memorize the word, baker. Which person do you think will have an easier time with memorization? The one who has to memorize the name of the word? If a person had to memorize the word, "baker," without creating a mental image, he or she would be unable to remember it. However, if he or she can think of an image of a baker, then they will undoubtedly have an easier time remembering the word. Baker has many connotations that we can connect to our memory. When we hear the word, "baker," we can associate it with the Pillsbury doughboy with a white hat on and flour all over his hands. What's more, we could smell the bread from a bakery and how we can visualize an image of a bakery. If we use this visual cue, then we could easily remember a person's name using the word association of baker.

Here's another example of how we can train our brains with word association. Take the name: Taylor. You are the CEO of a consulting company and see hundreds of people every day. And perhaps, you meet different customers all the time. But there's one problem: you don't remember names and faces. You struggle to remember the most basic of names. So, what you do is develop a technique for remembering the names and faces of the people you meet every day. Your customer is named Michael Taylor. Michael is pretty simple to remember, but the last name, Taylor, is a little harder to retain. Michael Taylor is a fashion expert, and he comes to you for advice about his clothing business. You're able to remember his last name now because Taylor could be spelled like "tailor," which also deals with clothing. In your mind, you can paint the image of a "tailor" at a store with lots of clothing. And then, voila... there you have it. The image is there, and you can now remember the name Michael Taylor because you have created a visual space that can remember the name, and you can also pair it with a face. That is the feat of visual and spatial memory.

Making Information Meaningful

The art of making your memory better is finding ways to connect ideas in your brain to match up meaningfully. Things without a context need to be put together so that your mind can easily picture what you're talking about. Our brains are designed to think contextually. Therefore, it is crucial that we find ways of connecting ideas to form a whole. Then, we can visualize what we are talking about.

Example

Creating meaningful experiences is essential for our physical and spiritual well-being. The more meaning we can find within our lives, the more experiences we can remember. Recall a time when you went on a trip with your parents, and where you were given free time to do whatever you wanted to. Think about the freedom that your parents provided you with. What did you do with it? How did you use it? Pondering on these experiences will make them more memorable. When you reflect on the experiences you have had, you can recall them more clearly and vividly. It's important to create amazing times you can never forget.

Create a Memory Palace

Using the technique of the Ancient Greeks, we advise you to create a memory palace, which is an edifice of your memory. Imagine that your memory is a large building that contains memories of different things. Visualize the palace of your memory and the different spaces within it that hold vital information about your life. This allows you to be spatially and visually oriented so that you will be able to better remember moments in your life. Imagine that you are Cicero and are invited to give a TED talk. You have to do all of it by memory and must use the technique that was used by the Greeks. So, how are you going to do that? By creating that visual palace. Let's look at an example below.

Close your eyes. Imagine that you are at the door of your house. Then, walk inside of it. You see the Cookie Monster dancing with his friends in your living room. Turn right, and you see Britney Spears, scantily dressed, dancing, and singing, "Hit Me Baby One More Time" on your coffee table. You also see Dorothy, Toto, the Tinman, Lion, and Scarecrow that are walking along the Yellow Brick Road that is coming out from the wall. Together, they are singing, "We're Off to See the Wizard." Then, you go into the kitchen where you see Martha Stewart cooking her famous turkey dinner. You can smell the turkey roasting in the oven. She is sauteing the garlic and onions to make her vegetable casserole. Then, you go to your bedroom, where you see Snoop Dogg, who is rapping up a storm on your bed. Finally, you come back outside and see Katy Perry, who is singing her hit song, "Firework," with fireworks shooting in the background.

Now open your eyes. You may not have been able to

remember all of those images in order, but you can put the different ideas together in your mind. With different bits of information, you're able to recall different moments that you thought about based on the various images that you are assembling in your mind, based on your background knowledge of the information presented. This is a crucial way that memory training works. It involves actively training your mind to create images using your existing memory and association of those thoughts. Then, and only then, can you remember the story better than before.

Remember Using Pictures

Essentially, what all of this is telling us is that we can best remember things if we put an image to them. We learn best when we can visualize what we're talking about. This is the primary way that we can go forward with our lives because we need an essential means of relating to the information that we receive every day.

How is this going to help you with your life? Remembering using pictures is going to help you remember everything. Gone are the days when you will forget your car keys. You can find ways to remember that, too. You will be able to remember all kinds of information from phone numbers to decks of cards, among other things. All of this will help you achieve greater career success. You will be the person everyone looks up to for crucial information because your memory will provide you with a vast deposit of the vital information to progress. You will also be well-respected by everyone in your company or workplace.

If you apply this method of training your memory, you will be able to remember many different kinds of things. You will revolutionize your life, because you will finally be able to remember all the things that you thought you had forgotten, and it will be an incredible time. You'll develop life skills that you can use for the rest of your life. Think of how you want to store up critical information in your mind that you never want to forget. Think about that graduation day for your son's college degree or your wedding. These are unforgettable experiences that you don't want to ever forget. But you also want to retain key details from each of these important events so that you can store up the treasures within your mind. Too much information becomes jumbled in a mass that can easily forget things. We can be incredibly forgetful people. But if we can apply the tenets of memory development, then we can change how we develop our memory and train ourselves to remember all of life's important events.

Conclusion

From this chapter, we have been able to show you how to train your memory so that you can remember words and other vital bits of information. It is about visualizing what you're talking about. You have to paint a picture in your mind of the different pieces of a puzzle. Your memory is like a building, where you have to reconstruct the images to form the parts of your consciousness. Each part functions differently but reveals the character of your memory, which becomes more real and vivid with time. By visualizing critical bits of information, you can memorize many different things, including phone numbers, names, faces, statistical data, among other things. You will not forget things like your car keys, what date it is, etc., because you can visualize those things in your mind. Additionally, you will be able to remember names and faces, because you can create a word picture of the name in your mind while associating it with a common word in everyday life. This is revolutionary training that you can use today and for the rest of your life.

Step 2: Use the Military Method

Our brains cannot wholly capture every detail of our lives. They are not cameras. Some people are born with better memories than others. Those who have extraordinary memory talent are called "eidetikers," but even these people may have trouble remembering necessary information because their brains are not entirely photographic ("Eidetic memory," n.d.). You may think, "Oh, I am so forgetful, and I cannot even remember the way to my house." The good news is that you can train your brain to remember the details of anything. In the previous chapter, we looked at how you can prepare your brain to think of different images and word associations. That is one of the best ways of general training. In this chapter, we are going to look at how to use the military method to produce some good results.

The military is continually doing advanced and crazy impressive research on different things, including psychic spies, objective viewing, and photographic memories (Boureston, n.d.). The military has trained millions of soldiers in how to remember coordinates, maps, etc. So, why don't we give it a shot? Let's use some tested military techniques to remember some details and see how it affects our abilities.

This method will teach you how to train your brain to have a photographic memory but also a good memory that remembers a lot of useful details. It is training you can do at home. Here are the steps you can take to do that.

Disclaimer

Before we go into how to use the military method, it is vital that we let you know that this method will take an extended time to develop; it won't happen overnight. Give yourself at least one month to do this experiment. It must be practiced every day. If you miss a day, then you may have to start all over again. Therefore, it is crucial that you find some time to do this every day, so make time for it in your schedule.

Steps to Enact the Military Method

The following steps outline how to successfully train your memory using the military method (Boureston, n.d.).

Step 1: Find a dark room that has no windows and where you can turn off all the lights. You need to be in a place where you won't have any distractions. But you have to have a bright lamp that hangs over the room. A bathroom would be an ideal place to do this.

Step 2: Sit down in a position where you can quickly turn on and off the light without having to leave your seat. Then, find a sheet of paper and cut a rectangular hole through it that is the size of a paragraph in a book.

Step 3: Take your book or the item you're attempting to memorize and cover it up with a sheet of paper that only allows you to see one paragraph.

Create a reasonable distance between you and the book so that when you open and close your eyes, you will be able to see and concentrate on the words immediately.

Step 4: Turn off the lights and allow your eyes to get used to the dark surrounding. Then, turn the light on for a nano-second and then turn it off again. At this point, you will have an image imprinted into your memory of the material that was placed in front of your eyes.

Step 5: If the memory of this text is fading, then turn the light on again for a nano-second and then stare back at the text.

Step 6: Continue doing this until you're able to remember all the words in the paragraph in the correct sequence.

If you're doing this step the right way, you will be able to visualize the text in your mind and read all the images of the text, as if it were right in front of you, because your memory has visually imprinted these images in your mind, much like a photograph.

Practice this once a Day for 15 minutes for one month.

You must be able to commit to this practice once a day for one month. Try to do it for 15 minutes a day, and you will be able to recall the information from any text. It will be amazing.

As you train your mind, you will be able to visualize different pieces of text and apply this principle to your daily life. It will help you so much more in your ability to do all things effectively.

Using the Military Method to Help with Memory-- Practical Example: Ron White, Two-Time USA Memory Champion

In a YouTube video, Ron White, Two-Time Memory Champion, explained how he got coached by a former Navy SEAL named TC Cummings to help him get the goal that he wanted to achieve (Ron White Memory Expert, 2016). Using five different military techniques, White could achieve his goal and went on to win the championship, but he did it through a lot of hard work and dedication to developing his memory.

Although White was not a Navy SEAL, he could learn a lot from what the military guys were doing in their training, because they helped him gain confidence in himself and his abilities to do great things. Here are some highlights that he wanted to emphasize as you are training your military memory style.

1. "The more you sweat in times of peace, the less you bleed in times of war."

This was a principle that he applied to his life as he was preparing to train his memory because he knew that he had to put himself through adverse circumstances to achieve his goal. When you're training for memory competitions or different things, it's essential for you to prepare your memory for war, instead of for times of peace, because chances are, you will have to undergo traumatic experiences in your life. Our lives are not easy peasy. We have to undergo some harsh realities that impact who we are as people. Therefore, it is crucial that we find ways to train ourselves in the less than ideal conditions because you never know when your health will go south or when you will encounter a traumatic, life-altering situation.

White illustrated this point by saying that he was going to train underwater in cold weather in January with a deck of cards and scuba gear. He memorized decks of cards while swimming underwater. It was a difficult task, but he was able to do it because he was facing the elements, even when it was not during a "wartime." Therefore, he was able to train much better than if he had trained under normal conditions.

2. Develop a Positive Mindset: Winning Frame of Mind

Secondly, if you want to be good at memorizing something, whether that is for a test or a memory competition, you must have a positive mindset and adopt a "winning" mentality that can recall all the experiences that you have had. Think about the high school debate team competition that you won, the model UN best delegate in committee award you received, or other achievements that you had during your childhood and in young adulthood. And then, pump yourself up so you will be able to achieve all the things you set out to do.

3. Set Small Goals for Your Memorization

If you want to memorize 20 decks of cards a day, do that. Start by learning a short text a little bit each day, and you will see results. For example, a man could memorize an entire chapter of Moby Dick each day by creating a memory palace and was able to do it very quickly over time. But it took him training and work to do it (Vox, 2016).

Step by step, you will be able to achieve the goal you set out to do. But you will have to put in the time and energy because nothing happens instantly. Everything requires a certain amount of patience and perseverance for it to work.

In Christian or religious circles, memorizing sacred texts is an important practice. Give yourself a few excerpts or verses to remember every day, and you will see how much you can learn and grow from this experience. It will be fantastic.

4. Always Face the Consequence of Not Hitting a Goal

Even though we may set goals that we want to achieve, we may not always reach them, and every time, we should set some form of consequence for ourselves, because that will be an essential part of our training. Losing is a consequence that can happen, but we have to give ourselves some form of small punishment, such as standing under cold water for two minutes, especially if we do not like cold water thrown at us.

It may be easy to brush it under the rug and not do anything about it, but we need to find ways of facing the consequences of our actions because every step that we take will have some result sooner or later. Therefore, the sooner we accustom ourselves to the consequences of not attaining our goal, the better off we will be.

5. Train Your Memory Every Day, Even When You Don't Feel Like It

The critical aspect of training is doing it every single day in preparation for an event, such as a big test or a competition. You cannot stop training simply because you're tired or don't feel like it. That is just not the way it works. You must train even on the days that you don't feel like continuing with it. It is vital to develop the discipline to do things militarily because you will do it regardless if you're feeling well or not. White had to go through this with his trainer. He was feeling sick and said to his trainer, Cummings, "TC, I'm sick. I cannot come in to train." TC told him that he had to train and that he was going to teach anyway. Even while sick, White had to complete his training. Just because you're sick or not feeling well doesn't mean you can skip training. Like I mentioned in point #1, you have to "face the music," even when you're not feeling up to speed about something.

On the day of the competition, White had another seemingly impossible obstacle. He wasn't sick, but he wasn't under the right conditions to succeed in the memory competition. Rather than being sick this time, he had only gotten 45 minutes of sleep the night before, so he had been up all night. Lack of sleep can pose a big problem to some people, and clearly, it was something that White struggled with, given that he had not received adequate rest the night before. But here's the thing: he had trained for this. He had spent months preparing for this moment, and he wasn't going to let lack of sleep stop him from achieving his goals. Therefore, he went after it with all he had. And it was incredible to see the end result.

Conclusion

To sum everything up, using the military method for memory training is going to greatly aid you as you seek to develop your mental concentration and retention of information. Using the dark room method is a great way to help you visualize information and graphically imprint the news in your mind in surprising ways. It will also increase your ability to concentrate on whatever it is you're doing, whether that is studying for a test, preparing for a memory competition, or getting ready for a speech for a conference. The more you train well in advance of the event, the better off you will be. You will feel the difference in all of these circumstances. Retention of information is a skill to be mastered; it is not a talent or gift. It is something that everyone can acquire and get better at. You must work toward your goal of memorizing essential information. That will be a necessary part of your development and experience in your life. If you do not focus on memorization, you won't be able to get to your goal. Therefore, it is crucial that you set some objectives for your life, as you seek to do all things well, during your studies and training. Setting goals will be an essential aspect that prepares you to enact a plan. You should give yourself a lot of pep talk because that will encourage you and give you a positive self-concept that will help you continue even in spite of the challenges.

The military mindset is an integral part of the training process to make you a better person. You have to train as if you are in a state of war. Not every day is going to be great. You will have to operate under challenging conditions. It will be hard. There are stressful and traumatic events that take place every day. You have to prepare yourself for those times. Likewise, you have to do all you can to keep training, even when you don't feel like it. A crucial part of developing a good memory is having the discipline to train even when you're not up for it. You must also persevere when times are complicated, and often, that takes doing things that will be hard whenever you're feeling under the weather. The show must go on. You cannot just let illness or fatigue keep you down. You must do everything in your power to keep going and don't give up whenever times get hard. It is crucial that you do this and get better at what you do. To succeed on a test or competition, you have to be prepared to "face the music," even when the conditions are not perfect. If you have prepared well and have trained to the best of your ability, you may still have a bad day. The trick is to not let these things get in the way and faze you when you have to perform.

Step 3: Improving Your Photographic Memory Diet

Maybe you want to dive into that big steak with pommefrites. But before you do that, you have to examine the fact: diet can influence our overall mental and psychological well-being. The more unhealthy foods we eat, the more likely we are to develop diseases like dementia as we age ("Boost your memory," 2012).

The steak that you want to bite into is rich in saturated fat, which can elevate your blood levels and give you unhealthy cholesterol levels. This harmful cholesterol is not only known to hurt your heart and other vital organs, but it can also harm your brain ("Boost your memory," 2012).

How is Memory Connected to Diet?

Diet is an essential aspect of what we consume every day. There is some truth to the adage: "you are what you eat," because we are the sum of the things that we consume from day to day. Therefore, it is crucial that we feed our minds with ideas that will be helpful and beneficial to our overall well-being. Otherwise, we will end up feeling weak and tired, which is not useful for our overall health. The things we need to limit in our diet include cholesterol, blood sugar, and blood pressure levels because these are necessary to protect our memory ("Boost Your Memory," 2012).

We should also be mindful about stocking up on healthy fats, which will help us to preserve memory. This includes mono and polyunsaturated fats, which are contained in foods like olive oil, fish, and nuts. These foods are also known to prevent dementia from Alzheimer's disease and mild cognitive impairment (MCI), which is a type of memory loss that appears right before dementia ("Boost Your Memory," 2012).

The foods of the Mediterranean diet are particularly useful for helping with memory. Here are some examples of them: fruits, vegetables, whole grains, and olive oil. Fish are also good foods for memory. Additionally, moderate alcohol consumption can help raise levels of healthy high-density lipoprotein (HDL) cholesterol and lower a person's resistance to insulin. Insulin resistance can lead to dementia ("Boost Your Memory," 2012.).

Sample Memory Diet

Breakfast

- Whole grain toast with fresh berries and almonds; or
- 8 oz. Greek yogurt that has berries spread over top of it.

Lunch

- Greek Mediterranean salad with grilled chicken strips; or
- Whole-grain pasta with hummus and cherry tomatoes.

Dinner

- Baked salmon with tomatoes and olives, spinach, raisins, and pears; or
- Grilled chicken breast with garlic and lemon, asparagus.

Even though some foods have been proven to protect memory, research has still not proven which foods can enhance our memories. We know what a heart-healthy diet looks like, but we don't exactly know what a brain-healthy diet is. However, doctors are trying to find the correlation between brain foods and heart-healthy foods ("Boost Your Memory," 2012). Eating heart-healthy diets low in saturated fat can help decrease the risk of diabetes and obesity, conditions that have been linked with memory loss

A Heart-Healthy Diet Can be a Brain-Healthy Diet

Here are some foods you should consider adding to your diet so that you can get the benefit of a heart-healthy diet, which can also help the development of your brain.

- Fruits and veggies
- Whole grain foods and pasta
- Beans and nuts
- Extra virgin olive oil (EVOO)
- Limited amounts of red meat
- Moderate consumption of alcohol (beer or wine)

Diets have been shown to significantly impact our ability to perform different tasks cognitively. Therefore, it is crucial that we find ways to improve our diet, because that will affect how we eat, how we live our lives, and how we get the proper nutrition that is necessary to living a healthier lifestyle. Going to McDonald's every week may seem like a temptation that many of us are faced with, and we may not think much about the consequences of our actions. However, it is true that a diet rich in unhealthy unsaturated fats and oils is not going to help our minds to think more clearly or efficiently. Consequently, our thinking may be impaired by it. But when we eat healthily, our entire body can feel a difference, including our brain. More blood can flow to the brain, giving it more energy and sustenance, which is necessary to feel at our best. No more trying to mask everything with caffeine and sugar highs, which can cause us to crash. If we adopt a healthy diet, we will be able to do much better and get the results that we desire in our life. And our memory will improve because we are taking care of our bodies by getting the proper nutrition. I know it's tempting to try to simply grab a meal out of convenience, especially when we are super swamped with things to do. But we must keep in mind that our lives depend on a certain level of self-care that enables us to do all the things that we want to do for ourselves and keep our bodies in tip-top shape.

The Foods and Drinks that We Recommend You Try for a Better Memory

You may be wondering, "what kinds of things can I eat to get my memory up to speed with the various things I must do?" We have some ideas for you here.

Coffee

Many of us rely on our morning coffee to get us through the day. If you are one of these people, know that coffee is very good for you. The two main aspects of coffee, caffeine and antioxidants, are helpful for your brain. Additionally, caffeine in coffee can help us in a number of ways, including making us more alert by blocking adenosine, which is a chemical that makes us drowsy. Additionally, coffee releases feel-good chemicals, such as serotonin. It also allows a person to concentrate more on what they are doing in that moment. Additionally, if you drink coffee for a long period, you reduce your risk of Parkinson's disease and Alzheimer's (Jennings, 2017). Sounds like a great plan to down your next cup of coffee, right?

Coffee is one of the best creations on the planet. Drinking coffee also helps your digestive system to process various foods. It can help us remember things more clearly, because we can focus on what is important to us. On the other hand, it is also important to watch that our consumption of it doesn't get out of control. Moderation is always the best way to go forward.

Turmeric

The yellow spice found in curry powder has many benefits for the brain. Curcumin can enter the brain directly and do good things for our brain cells. It has a strong antioxidant; which Alzheimer's patients can benefit from. Additionally, it helps with depression, so that you don't feel too down during your day. It also encourages cell growth, which helps with memory in older people. If you want to benefit from using curcumin, you should add it to different dishes or make turmeric tea (Jennings, 2017).

Broccoli

Have you ever thought that broccoli might be very good for you? Well, it is. It is filled with antioxidants. Broccoli has high vitamin K content, which has been linked to having a better memory. It also has compounds that may help guard the brain from damage over time (Jennings, 2017).

Dark Chocolate

Dark chocolate and cocoa powder contain a lot of compounds, including antioxidants and caffeine, which improve the function of your memory. It contains flavonoids, which help the brain to learn and memorize different pieces of information. In one study, researchers showed that these compounds may help with mental decline in older people. Chocolate also boosts our mood, because it gives positive feelings. It is uncertain as to why it makes people happy, but perhaps it has to do with the yummy flavor (Jennings, 2017).

Oranges

Oranges have a lot of vitamin C, which offers a lot of health benefits, including preventing mental decline in older age. When we eat enough foods containing vitamin C, we can also protect ourselves against Alzheimer's disease. Vitamin C helps in the improvement of our brain's overall health (Jennings, 2017).

Eggs

Eggs contain several nutrients that help strengthen our brain, including choline, which helps with mood regulation and memory. Two studies have shown that people who take in more choline have improved memory and cognitive functioning (Jennings, 2017). Getting your choline dose can come from simply eating the egg yolk, which is where you can find most of the healthy stuff.

Green Tea

Similar to coffee, green tea also has caffeine, which improves people's alertness, cognitive functioning, and memory. Additionally, it allows people to concentrate better on the tasks they have to do. One of the chemicals that is found in green tea is L-theanine, which makes you feel less anxious and more relaxed (Jennings, 2017).

Try Diets that Include More Fat and Less Carbs

There are lots of diet plans out there, and not every one of them is helpful, but if you want, you can try out a diet plan that will help you achieve your weight loss goals. For example, you could try the Keto diet, which is rich in fat and protein but low on the carbs and sugar. Carbs and sugar can give us energy for short periods, but then they deplete us of energy and causes us to fall into a deep drowsiness, which makes it difficult for us to concentrate. The more we eat these foods, the more likely we will experience weight gain and other unwanted effects. Moreover, we want to eat foods that will give us energy throughout the day and not cause us to crash. Additionally, when you can provide your body with more fat, you can store that energy and make intermittent fasting a part of your routine.

Intermittent Fasting

Integrating fasting in your diet is one way that you can improve your cognitive performance, because you are able to concentrate more on your studies, and it is easy to implement in your lifestyle. If you adopt a diet that can carry you over for hours, it will help you to be able to start intermittent fasting, which has proven health benefits. Try it out. You will see that you can develop some energy and stamina from doing intermittent fasting, and you can also boost your cognitive performance.

Moderate Drinking, So You Can Remember More

Alcohol has been shown to help us to forget the difficult times and remember more of the good times. It affects a gene called D2-like receptor, which records memory and encodes it as pleasant or unpleasant. Alcohol can make us forget the awkward moments in our lives and produces a reward mechanism that we can experience every time we drink.

However, it can also make us prone to forget things easily (Kekatos, 2018).

Many people, especially youth and young adults, are prone to abuse alcohol in ways that are quite destructive to their health and memory. Not only does excessive drinking cause problems with controlling one's behavior and having a rough time out and about at the pub, but it also causes problems for memory retention that make it increasingly difficult to remember things of our past. It can make a person, especially forgetful and lose their memory. Think about it. When a person drinks to excess, they are unlikely to be able to remember anything that went on the previous night, because the effect of alcohol causes problems with remembering events. Excessive drinking is likely to impair cognitive functioning for a while after the excessive drinking, which can make it challenging to function the next day and be able to do all the activities that you set out to do.

Case Study

John realized that his diet was not helping his overall health. He ate out all the time and did not watch the calories he was consuming. Consequently, he felt like he was gaining weight all the time, and he couldn't control it. John knew that his habits were unhealthy, but he didn't want to do anything about it. Then, one day, he got the diagnosis: diabetes. He was shocked by this discovery and felt that he had to do something about it. His doctor and nutritionist gave him some tools to get back on the right path. He chose a steady diet of fruits and vegetables and protein, which would help him to maintain a healthy weight. Additionally, he would consume more fats and less carbs. After a few weeks, John noticed that his energy levels were higher. Additionally, he was able to better remember details about his life. He didn't feel like he was losing his mind. He had a better memory, which served him well in his job, as a sales assistant.

Conclusion

Diet is an important part of our memory development. If we don't have a good diet, how can we expect to have a good memory? We need to watch all the foods that we put in our mouths, because that will enable us to live a healthier life. Don't procrastinate any longer. You should try your best to get your diet plan on the right path, so you can plan out your life. Start by getting on a plan that allows you to know exactly what you'll eat every day. Then, you can watch the calorie and fat content of the various foods you consume. After a few weeks, you will notice how much your diet affects your memory, and you might just be able to remember all the details of your life. Let diet be part of your cognitive training for a better memory and a better you.

Step 4: Sleeping for Memory's Sake

The average American is living his or her life in chronic sleep deprivation. We are living a life of overdrive. Our lives are going by really fast. We are working harder than ever, taking less vacation time than before, and are trying to earn more money than before. And it is all seemingly an endeavor that we want to become more prosperous. But what if I told you the secret to living a happier life lies in getting more z's and less consumption of caffeine and coffee that keeps your mind and body awake at all times of the night. In this chapter, we are going to go into the ways that getting good sleep is going to help you to develop a better memory, a photographic memory.

Why Good Sleep is Important

We spend over a third of our lives sleeping. We might not often think about why we sleep, but we see the outward manifestation of the benefits of sleeping. We feel more energetic and alert and are able to concentrate better on the tasks that we are doing. Without sleep, our cognitive functions suffer, and we perform less well ("Why Do We Sleep," n.d.).

For us to fully appreciate sleep, we must acknowledge that sleep is a vital function of our bodies. We should consider it just as important as eating. We know that we need food and nutrients to survive. There is no way we can live our lives without it. It helps us grow, develop, repair broken tissues, and work well. It is a physical process that requires that we ingest the things that we need to keep going every day. But you might be thinking to yourself, "sleeping is just not as important as eating." But it is a vital part of our bodily processes.

Good sleep leads us to a place of physical and mental restoration of all the things that are impairing our brains and causing it to get tired, overworked, among other things. Sleep allows our internal bodily functions to slow, as our body rests and recovers from different stressors and situations that can wreak havoc on it. In our modern world, we put so much pressure on our body to do things that it can only do well if it sleeps well at night. We continue to go without sleep and try to function without too much of it, which causes anxiety, depression, and other mental health conditions. It also leads us to be more tired and unable to cognitively perform the deeds that we must do during our day.

The Theories Behind Sleep

Although much is known about the inherent health benefits of sleep, little has been understood as to why we sleep, but there are some theories. One postulate is the inactivity theory, which comes from an evolutionary instinct where animals would sleep to remain still out in the wild and protect themselves from predators during the day ("Why Do We Sleep", n.d.).

Another theory talks about how people can conserve energy and reduce energy consumption so that they can be saved for another day. Still, another talk about how our body needs to restore certain aspects of what is lost during the day time. When we are awake, the neurons in the brain can produce adenosine, which can lead to feelings of fatigue. This feeling is blocked when we consume caffeine and keep ourselves alert. When we are awake, this hormone continues to amass in our brain and remain high until it is cleared out during sleep. When we sleep, our bodies can shake out the adenosine from the mind. It allows us to feel a lot better the next day when we wake up first thing in the morning. Our mind and body feel refreshed from the effects of sleep ("Why Do We Sleep," n.d.).

Sleeping is vital for our well-being because we could not function without it. If we were to stop sleeping and not get adequate rest every night, then we would cease to work well over time. With the passing time, we will become more fatigued and eventually wear down and burn out. The worst-case scenarios of sleep deprivation include sickness and burnout. These require continual recovery from the intensive periods that make sleep deprivation happen, and it can be extremely detrimental to our overall well-being not to get enough sleep.

What Does Sleep Do for Memory?

In addition to its necessity for our bodies to function properly, sleep functions in a significant way to help our memories as we rest our brains at night. Research has shown that sleep can help a person to learn and retain things in their memory well. When a person is sleep-deprived, they will not be able to learn efficiently and will be prone to forget things. Also, sleep is responsible for the consolidation of memory, which allows a person to learn new information ("Why Do We Sleep," n.d.).

For a person's memory to properly function, different steps must be followed. First, the brain must acquire new information. Then, it must consolidate the data during which the memory can become stable. Finally, the brain must be able to recall the data after it has been stored within a person's brain. We can acquire and remember the different parts of things in our wakefulness. But studies have shown that sleep is the state in which memory consolidation occurs ("Why Do We Sleep," n.d.).

What we must realize is that our memories are cemented into us while we are sleeping. Whenever we study for a test, we rely on the storage of those memories into our brain so that we can readily access the information when we are awake and taking the test. This is mostly done unconsciously without us being aware of it. There is a lot of wisdom in getting proper rest before doing something big like a presentation, test, or competition. If we don't get good rest, we won't be able to perform well for these events. That doesn't mean it's impossible to do well if we don't get adequate rest before the event. But it just cognitively hinders our brains in their ability to do things well. Anyone can cram a bunch of information into their brain the night before a big test and expect to get a good result on the test. Short-term memory is more comfortable to access, as we can remember things that we just looked at, but it is very likely that we will completely forget the information that we have crammed for right after the test. Therefore, the cramming method is very inefficient and does not enable people to get the right results for their memory. Instead, it splits our knowledge into fragments and makes it much easier to forget.

Example of Korea: Cramming Schools, Rote Memorization, and the Absence of Sleep

You're transported to the modern city of Seoul, Korea. It is a beautiful city and metropolis that resembles New York City. Many people are residing in this area, at least 10 million people. Go to a place called Gangnam, where you might see a bunch of BMWs or Rolls Royce cars driving by. An evening out here may cost you 100,000 won ($100 USD) because you're in the ritzy area of Seoul. Now, go to a place called Daechi-dong in Seoul, where there are hundreds of English schools in the area filled with students, who are studying for the Korean SAT, TOEFL, and TOEIC tests. Welcome to the English education culture of Korea, a place where many people are intensively studying English, but wait, are they really learning English, or just cramming?

If you go to an English academy (or in Korean: hagwon), you will find thousands of students cramming for their tests and memorizing lists of hundreds of vocabulary words. Korean English teachers give their students 50 words per day to study. On other days, they study 100 words a day or even 500 words a week. They study hard and memorize words in English and Korean. Daily word tests abound, and students are continually cramming and trying to jam the information into their heads, much to no avail because their teenage brains are still developing and are cementing only fragmented knowledge. The truth is, this method is inefficient for helping the cognitive development of teenagers, as they go through the period of adolescence and early adulthood. Children and adolescents are marred by a period of intensive angst by studying English because they are using a rote memorization method.

What's more, students in Korea are not getting enough sleep. They are sleeping a lot less every night. They are getting 4-5 hours of sleep. They go to school from the early morning all the way up to 3 or 4 in the afternoon. Then, they typically go to a separate English academy from 4 pm to 10 pm and continue studying until 1 or 2 in the morning, at which point they finally go to sleep for the night. This is the typical life of a Korean teenager, "studying" English all the time, and getting no sleep. There are dire consequences to the mental health of Korean teenagers, as they suffer through and get little to no sleep. The repercussions are important. Even after studying so much, close to 14 hours a day, the students are not able to retain the information given to them. They forget everything after the test. After all the studying, they are left with a little more than an exam result to show for their studying for hundreds of hours every month. The cram school industry is a lucrative business because of the exploitative nature of both teachers and students.

What does Korea teach us about sleep? The enormous amounts of sleep deprivation in Korea should hint that sleep is crucial to academic success. However, it also shows that though students are intensively test-focused and can be ultimately successful in getting the result for the test from endlessly studying at all hours, their cognitive development is severely impacted, because they are cramming large amounts of information within a short period of time. They are not really learning the information, although they are constantly bombarded with the information. Consequently, they are unable to completely process everything that they are studying because their brain has no time to process the information that they have visibly. But one of the key reasons is that they are not getting any sleep in the process, so their bodies are wearing out and they become very unhealthy. They do not have a properly developed brain, which makes it a lot harder for them to learn anything, much less English.

Sleep Deprivation Has Dire Consequences for Our Memory

Now, we should be aware that sleep deprivation will have dire consequences on our memory development. If we go without sleep daily, we will lose our memories, and it may be difficult to fully recover from these periods of our lives. Rest has a restorative power that enables us to fully function and recover from different situations in our lives that causes energy loss. However, we must find ways to regain our sleep because our bodies need it. Our memory also needs it, because, to recover the memories that are stored deep within us, we must sleep and rest our minds. Our dreams demonstrate a lot of what our consciousness can consolidate, so the more that we dream, the more we're able to see that our bodies are restoring themselves and filling up our memories with information that can be stored for the rest of our lives.

How to Up Your Memory and Enable You To Remember: Sleep!

So, what is our recommendation for how you can recover your memory? Sleep! Seriously, get some shut-eye now. If you're staying up late, don't do it. Try to get in bed earlier. Don't allow yourself to consume caffeine and keep you up at all hours endlessly. Rest your mind, and don't do anything that requires too much work. Rest is under-emphasized in this economy. Everything seems to be about productivity and how much work you can produce for your employer. But we have to mindful of the fact that we cannot operate this way. Our brains are not meant to operate this way. They must have sleep to properly function, so getting enough sleep at night is going to help you and your ability to remember things. If you are continually relying on caffeine to get you through the day, you skip out on catching your z's every night and get 4-5 hours of sleep, and you go into the office with a gallon of your coffee with an extra shot of espresso. But this is not the way to live your life. You should get your daily dose of sleep because that is going to make every difference in how you can live a better life and live with a better work-life balance. But it is also the key to unlocking your memory, because, the more you reste, the more your brain will be able to consolidate and store the knowledge that it collects daily, which causes us to dream at night. Don't you want to have more dreams at night? It will help you a lot in your life.

Case Study

Jane was a conscientious student, although she didn't always know how to study. Her life was filled with cramming for exams, and often, she would stay up until 3am to do her work. Unfortunately, she did not know how to manage her time well, so she ended up having many problems with concentration in school. When she arrived to class, she was exhausted and was unable to listen to the teacher. She tried to mindlessly take notes, but all she wanted to do was put her head down and sleep. Her teachers noticed that she was having trouble, and they wanted to help her. One teacher told her, "Jane, you need to get some shut-eye at night. I can tell you're not sleeping a lot, and that is affecting your ability to focus in my class. You need to adopt a normal bed time and follow it religiously." Jane didn't realize that what she had been doing was affecting how she could do her homework. Although Jane tried hard to study at night, she ended up passing out from the stress of everything. She started doing what her teacher told her to do, and after a month or two, she was able to concentrate in class. No longer was she falling asleep in class like she used to. Additionally, she was able to score higher on her tests, because she could remember what she had studied the night before. It helped her a lot.

Conclusion

To sum up, it is clear that we absolutely must both eat well and rest our heads at night. That is going to be one of the only ways that we can recover our memories. But especially in the case of photographic memory, we must get enough sleep at night to consolidate all the memories in our brains and do well with all things. If we catch some z's at night, we will be able to feel much better and have a healthier balance in our lives. That is crucial to our overall success, so when in doubt, just go to bed. Your memory will thank you and your whole body, too.

Step 5: Use Mnemonic Devices to Remember Almost Anything

In this chapter, I will discuss how we can remember almost anything using mnemonic devices, which can facilitate a better memory.

Our memories are meant to be shaped by the word associations that we form with them. We have to develop meaning by constructing images that are connected by some idea. One way that we can do this is through using mnemonic devices to remember things in our lives. Often, we don't remember things, because we don't understand how to train our minds to remember. Consequently, we forget things and try to rely on rote memorization. But as we have learned, this method is ineffective and fruitless. The thing that we need to focus on is how we can apply memory concepts to our lives and enact new ideas.

Mnemonic devices are something that have been used for a long time. Mnemonic comes from the Greek word, *mnemonikos*, which means to "to be mindful" ("Mnemonic," n.d.). Mnemonic devices enable a person to remember something better. It allows you to encode something within your memory so that you will be able to recall things on demand. Mnemonic devices have been used since the ancient Greeks, and they enabled people to have better memories.

Here are some examples of mnemonic devices:

The Method of Loci

The Method of Loci is a technique where you imagine yourself in a familiar place, such as your house or park. It is similar to the memory palace idea. And then you use the usual sites to store your memories. You read a list of words or concepts that require memorization and then you put each of these words in the locations of your familiar place. It will help you memorize almost anything. Then, you will be able to go back through this information in the future ("Memory and Mnemonic Devices," n.d.). It's a fantastic idea.

Acronyms

People have been using acronyms for a long time to remember different concepts. Think back to your high school algebra class, where you had to remember PEMDAS for the order of operations. Then, each time, you would go through it and say the order of operations in a math problem was: Parentheses, Exponents, Multiplication, Division, Addition, and Subtraction. I'm sure that after that high school algebra class, you have never forgotten how to do those operations. It is likely that you might be able to solve a simple arithmetic problem based on this strategy, as well. Sometimes, you can remember a person's name by simply writing out different words to describe that person. For example, take the example of a person named Daniel, you could construct meaning for that person's name simply by writing out an acrostic poem about that person.

- Daring
- Awesome
- Navigational
- Intelligent
- Expressive
- Language-oriented

Each of these qualities describes a specific person in mind, who is also a good friend of mine named Daniel. If I use this same acronym, I will be able to remember his name without any problem. It's better than rote memorization and also enables me to remember aspects of individuals in a way that helps me to get to know them better.

Creating a Memory Class (For Teachers)

For teachers, there is always consistent anxiety surrounding students names in a classroom. Teachers working in multicultural environments might also find that learning names is quite tricky and unmanageable. However, don't worry! You can do it! Remembering names in a classroom can be fun and exciting. One way is to visualize where each student is in the classroom and identify where they are in the room. Using a seating chart can help with this process, as we can visualize where the students are sitting in a classroom at any given time. The device of a seating chart can help people to remember names very fast and can bring a specific spatial dimension to learning and memorizing names of different students.

In Different Cultures: Use English names

English teachers in Korea are known for giving their students English names because they cannot correctly pronounce Korean names because of how incredibly complicated they are. This method is particularly useful for English teachers working in Korean universities, where you normally teach between 100 to 150 students per week in classes and have many different ways to remember the names. This is one of the ways to help a person remember a hundred names off the top of their head. Or better yet, you could also use a seating chart and use English names for some of the classes, while retaining the Korean names for the other courses. That helps, too. Either way, it allows you to develop a strong sense of understanding how to make the associations. Another thing a teacher may do is allow students to write their acrostics, which will enable you to understand the different aspects of the students personalities.

Rhymes

Another mnemonic device that people can use is the concept of a rhyme, which gets students to memorize long lists. It is commonly known that Shakespeare used blank verse and iambic pentameter with rhyme to make his lines easier to remember. Therefore, quoting Shakespeare should be feasible for most people in different capacities. There are various forms of rhymes that we use all the time to try to remember things. Let's look at several common examples of this.

- In fourteen hundred and ninety-two, Columbus sailed the Ocean Blue.

- All's well that ends well.

- Red sky in the morning, shepherd's warning.

Poetry, which is meant to be read aloud, often includes a rhyming component, because the sound of similar end rhymes enables people to remember the words of the verse more clearly and efficiently. This also makes reciting poetry from memory a particularly useful way of memorizing.

How Do You Memorize that Lengthy Poem? Make an Image of It in Your Mind

Have you ever wondered how people memorize long poems that have so many words? Well, it does not happen by merely staring at a page for a long time. No, remembering requires a whole unique way of visualizing how things happen on the page. When you learn a poem by heart, you memorize the sights and sounds that are coming off the page. You take in all five senses and then you're able to do it well. One way to do this is to imagine the image that you want to study using all five senses. For example, if you're studying a poem about snow, for example, then you can visualize what the snow tastes like, looks like, smells like, feels like, and sounds like. Think about all those things and construct the image in your mind.

Once you have studied the images and have made it real in your mind, then you can begin to memorize the poem. Again, the strategy is not rote memorization; instead, it is creating the image, so that it is a real image to you. If you cannot visualize it in your mind, then there is no way you'll be able to remember it. You will simply forget it. Unfortunately, this is the way the majority of people operate. They stare at a text for a long time and then try to reproduce it on a test. But then afterward, they forget everything. It's as if the memory never formed in their minds, and it is all because there was never a tangible image in the first place.

Case Study

Jeremy enjoyed reading poetry at home. He wanted to learn how to memorize various poems, because he wanted to perform at the next school poetry slam. So, he worked with all his might on memorizing, "The Highwayman" by Alfred Noyes. This was one of his favorite poems from high school and he wanted to challenge himself to recall the entire poem, while participating in the competition. He was able to remember a lot from the poem simply by remembering the sounds of the onomatopoeic words that he spoke out loud, as he was practicing. Here is an example of a section that he was able to memorize perfectly:

The Highwayman came riding-- Riding-- riding--The red coats looked to their priming! She stood up, straight and still. (Noyes, n.d.)

As he was memorizing these lines, he started to visualize everything from this scene and he walked through the whole poem. Then, he was able to graphically re-create the image, as he was reading the poem. Finally, he could speak the whole poem without looking at the words. During the poetry slam, he recited the whole poem by heart, and he received a thunderous applause.

How to Memorize Lines for the Next Town Play

Have you ever wondered how actors can memorize lines efficiently? Remember Linus in Charlie Brown Christmas: "I can't memorize these lines so quickly. Why do I have to be put through such agony?!" ("Tracy Stratford," n.d.). It may seem disturbing at the time to try to memorize lines to a play or for a movie, but the thing is, it is quite simple and easy to do. Learning lines is something that can be done quickly and fluidly, depending on how you do it. But you need to create some mnemonics for it, and then you're ready to go. Often, actors visualize the role that they are about to incarnate, and then they do it. It is quite amazing how they can pull it off so well. It helps that actors can actually "become" the roles that they are reading from a script. It all begins with reading but then as you act on stage or on screen, you create the character, and that helps the actors to remember. It is a full-body experience, in which everything is mnemonic in design so that the actors can easily recall the lines from the script and incarnate the characters that they were born to play.

Case Study: Jemima

Jemima was a theatre nerd. She absolutely loved to put on a show for people. But her memory was full of holes that it was hard for her to memorize her lines in plays. She would cram, and cram, and cram, all day long to be in the show. Because her memory was pretty spotty, the directors didn't want to give her critical parts of a play.

Consequently, she always received the supporting roles and sometimes even the extra roles. It was pretty awful. She felt bad. Jemima wanted to improve her memory, so she needed to train herself to develop her memory so she could land a leading role in a local play. After a while, Jemima started memorizing mnemonic devices, which enabled her to recall the information well. She put mnemonics in her daily routine so she could easily remember her lines to the play. When she came to the next audition, she nailed it. She could fully remember all her lines with complete success. It was a fantastic day, as she felt confident enough that she could say the lines backward due to her intensive studies the week leading up to the audition. It was a fantastic story.

Chunking and Organization

Another way that we can remember information, such as phone numbers, is by grouping and ordering the data into "chunks," which makes it easier to remember. We do this all the time to be able to retain our phone number. We say things in groups of three or four so that we can remember it better. The ten digits are broken up into three parts, allowing people to recognize the information quickly. Our brains are designed to remember things in small chunks, not in large quantities. Moreover, the more we feed our minds with information in fragments, the more likely we can retain stuff at the top of our heads. Our short-term memory is limited to seven items of information, and as we put everything into different groupings, our brain will have a faster and more effective recall of the data ("Memory and Mnemonic Devices," 2018).

Another way to remember is to use the organization method to sort all the information into individual categories, which allow us to remember all the details. This is a particularly useful way of doing it. When you can categorize the data, then you can put it in different places so that you can do all the things you want to do with the data. Then, you can divide it into lists that will make it easier for you to remember all of it.

Case Study: Jason

Jason loved to use his imagination. He had a unique ability to make things creative, including memorizing stories. As a young boy, he loved to memorize stories from books such as the Bible and the Quran. He had a spiritual orientation and wanted to do his best to discover different religions. The technique that he used to help him memorize was chunking various texts together and then memorizing each part of the story. Instead of staring straight at a text over a certain period of time, he chose to memorize it in parts. What he would do is take a story and break it into sections that he could quickly memorize. He would write out one of the religious stories and then cut the paper into pieces and later try to put everything together in order. As he did this using repetition, he was eventually able to remember the whole story. It was an amazing feat of the imagination, and it was all due to his industry and talent.

Do a Jingle or a Dance to Remember Things Well

Why not try doing a jingle or a dance to remember things? You could try to do the "Bone Dance" from Hannah Montana to remember the anatomy of your bones (Robinson, 2008). It is a full-body experience, wherein you memorize the different parts of the anatomy and then sing the words. It is quite amazing to recall. As I was watching this video, I could remember vividly watching this when I was younger, and it made my heart leap for joy because I knew the "Bone Dance." The jingle is stuck in my memory, although perhaps buried deep within the caverns of time.

Doing a jingle or a dance gives yourself a kinesthetic and audiovisual experience of the memory that you had of something. It becomes that much more real because you remember exactly how it sounded, how it looked, etc. And when you apply this to memorizing, say, the Periodic Table of the Elements, then you can do well to remember all the things that you need to. Many people have been doing this for ages. This is still a useful way to remember things. It's incredible how much you can recall because your muscle and audiovisual memory can give you fantastic recall. It makes you feel like you're superhuman.

Case Study

Henry always wanted to do better at memorizing things, and he tried to memorize the formulas to mathematics. He was not so good at math, because he had trouble with calculations. As a result, he tried with all his might to come up with ways to remember his multiplication tables. His mother helped him a little along the way, but he still struggled to remember how to multiply and divide numbers. But then, an idea came to him. He thought, "why don't I invent a jingle that can be used to help me remember all the multiplication tables?" Henry was gifted in music and knew a lot about composing, even at a very young age (he was about nine at the time). Like a little Mozart, he went to his keyboard and began to compose a jingle, and he could produce an amazing little work that he then combined with his multiplication tables. Afterward, he started singing the jingle and felt that he could enjoy his life more. By the time he had another multiplication test at school, he was able to score 100%. It was an amazing feat of the imagination and his photographic and musical memory.

Conclusion

What's in a memory? It is something that we can vividly and tangibly remember. How do we do that? Through making the associations that give us the sight and sound that our whole bodies can remember. Mnemonic devices give us that access because they give us clever and inventive ways to remember almost anything. If we use mnemonic devices, then we cannot forget all the things that we set our minds to, because our brains are built for associations. The more connections and associations that we can create with our brains, the better we will be able to remember. By training our minds to remember the minute details of our lives, then we can truly make the most of the memory that we do have of events. It allows us to be much more free to express ourselves and to experience remembrance and time regained. The best part of all of this is that we are open to express our deepest thoughts with the memories that we cherish and treasure all the days of our lives. Time is short, and we don't have a lot of it left before death. Therefore, it is crucial that we number our days and retain all memories so that we can treasure all the good times forever.

Step 6: Everyday Techniques: Use the Senses

In this chapter, we are going to talk about how you can use common techniques to be successful in making a mental picture of just about anything under the sun. Let's begin with using the five senses and seeing how that can help us.

How to Make Things Real: Create Absurd Images to Remember

One of the critical aspects of learning something is to make associations that are weird and outrageous to remember the details about it. Think of something along these lines: crying and screaming babies, sloshing through the snow, puddles of rain, buckets of butter. These are associations that use alliteration and the five senses to awaken your imagination. The more you're able to use your imagination, the better off you will be in remembering. So, you need to think of ways of remembering and use your imagination to get you started.

The human imagination is one of the greatest things on the planet, and it gives us the depth of insight, knowledge, and understanding of all the things around us. As long as we can form the mental images in our heads, the sky's the limit when it comes to producing mental models that can help us to have creative imaginations. We have been gifted with a vision that paints the world with possibilities and enlightens us with the best ideas of the future. At the same time, our imaginations can lead us too far off places, where we don't want to go, and to areas that are unhealthy and not needed. But, the human imagination can produce more ideas than we can think of, and it is because we have created a concept that keeps us going and enables us to come up with solutions to the world's problems.

Having a good imagination is going to help your memory, especially if you want to develop a photographic memory. Reading good books, watching movies, and other media will enable you to cultivate your imagination and make it into a useful tool that will produce good results. That is where you need to train your imagination in developing thoughts that can be beneficial and productive.

Case Study

Emily wanted to read more widely. She looked to the classics as her source of inspiration. All the while, she wanted to do her best in her studies. For a while, she painted and used her imagination. She realized she needed to paint the images of stories in her mind because she could not remember all the small details of things she read in the stories. So, she used her imagination more and more, and thus created more. She also resorted to writing down her thoughts as she painted. As a result, she concluded that she could remember more details from the stories that she was reading because she wrote everything down and also painted pictures of passages from the readings. It helped her to remember things more clearly. It was through these experiences she could recall the things that came to her mind from the various books she was reading. Emily was then able to improve her overall memory.

Things went well from that point onward.

Turn the Sounds of Names that We Learn into Images

Perhaps, you are learning names in a group, and you introduce yourself to a man named Jacob, and you think to yourself, "I've completely forgotten the name. How did I do that?" Then, perhaps you could tie Jacob to a Biblical character or to a person that you have already met by that name. Once you make these connections, it's easier to remember things, like in this case, someone's name. Or, maybe you introduce yourself to a woman named Melanie. You could think of her name and also think of the words "melon" and "knee." Sometimes, it is also helpful for you to think of visual images that connect to the people's names you're trying to remember. For example, if you know a man named Charlie, you can remember his name by referring to Charlie Chaplin, Charlie and the Chocolate Factory, or Charlie Brown. Soon enough, you'll be memory association professional.

Case Study

Mr. Park was an elementary school teacher. He worked in a private school in Seoul, South Korea, where he taught elementary school kids English for two hours weekly. Mr. Park struggled to remember most of his students names. He had a poor memory. But he was able to invent some devices, which enabled him to remember most of the names that he had on his class lists. First, he developed English names for all his kids so he could remember a list of twenty students in one class. Then, he retained the names of some of them in Korean. He was able to remember much faster with this method. He memorized the names of different students. For example, he could remember students named David based on the Davids he had taught before. But also, he thought of some famous people who were named David. He also learned the names of students with the months of the year. He was able to learn those names and apply them to memory quickly. Another child's name was Ellie, so when he looked at her, he thought to himself, "Ellie Goulding." It was by making these associations that Mr. Park was able to learn the names of all the students in his classes. It helped him a lot.

Use as Many of Your Senses As Possible

In your efforts to memorize, you should use as many of the senses as you possibly can, because this will enable you to accomplish almost any feat. For example, if you want to memorize the name of a man named Mike, you can visualize Mike with a microphone singing a karaoke song at night. Or better yet, you might imagine Michael Jordan slam dunking a hoop at a Chicago Bulls game in 1998. This can create a historical memory that you can enshrine within your memory bank. If you want to remember the name of a girl named Melanie, you can remember Melanie Hamilton, that "goodie-goodie" from "Gone with the Wind," who was Scarlett O'hara's rival and a woman of a pure heart.

Another example: think of the name, Harry. How do you remember a man named Harry? Think about Harry Potter, a wizard flying through space with a magic wand.

As for a woman, think of the name, Eve. Who do you think of when you hear the name, Eve? Maybe Eve in the Garden of Eden, who was tempted by the serpent and sinned alongside Adam? Or, perhaps you think of Eve with the homonym Yves Saint Laurent. Then, you immediately think of fashion and runways, and beautiful and handsome models, who are strutting their stuff with the latest fashion trend.

When It Comes to Numbers, Use the Same Method

Numbers often put us off, because we think, "I cannot memorize that many numbers. My memory is so bad." But we can apply the same principles to numbers that we do to names. For example, you might think of 0 as a donut hole. Or, you could remember 007 for James Bond or 00 for Ozzy Osbourne. Many people remember essential dates such as 9/11 for September 11 or May 4, May the Fourth be With You, Star Wars Day. You can use a lot of creativity to get yourself to remember different numbers. It is not so tricky, so give it a try.

Case Study

Jericho was not good at math or numbers, for that matter. He forgot his phone number and passcode to get into his house every day. Even though he stored the information in his phone, he still managed to forget all the information. As he was studying for his tests, he immediately forgot everything he had studied afterward because he was relying on his limited and faulty rote memorization skills. But then, he started thinking about the patterns he could form with the numbers and the different ways that he could remember different figures. It was difficult at first, but he soon started to realize that he could assign values to the various numbers. For example, he could think of 7 as the ideal number in different contexts. Jericho could also remember different figures with 6 because it represents the Greek ideal of perfection.

Another example is 747. If he ever saw this figure, he could instantly remember it, because he could conjure up the image of a 747 jet in his mind that was flying away to New Zealand.

Use Your Sensory Memory to Re-Create Experiences

Sensory memory is something that many actors use to recreate experiences they have had on stage and on the screen. This method is known as using affective memory, which is how you manipulate your experience to recreate an emotional experience in a character (Timoney, 2016). When actors recall their experiences, they can then demonstrate in the character they create on the screen. Here's an example of a situation that you could use with affective memory:

In this scene, you have been asked to think back of a time when you broke up with your girlfriend or boyfriend. Because the experience is fresh in your mind, then you have a good emotional trigger that will aid in remembering and then re-creating the experience.

As soon as you think of a specific memory, you can go through the experience in your head and think of the sights, sounds, and smells that you experienced then. For example, you can recall the smell of garlic bread in the restaurant you visited a few months ago, where you suddenly experienced pain in your stomach. The painful memory allows you to remember that experience. Later, when you are asked to perform a scene, you can simply think back to the smell of the garlic bread, and then all the sensations will bring the memory back to you.

Although we can be unaware of it, every memory we have uses one of the five senses. When we think back to an event, we often only remember sight and sound. But, if we engage all the senses, then we can remember vividly every aspect of the experience.

Case Study

You are invited to recall a memory where you were in a long-distance relationship with someone. You had been going out for a long time. Every once in awhile you meet with your significant other in each other's hometown. Say, your name is Kelsey and your boyfriend's name is Taylor. You meet Taylor at his house in Tulsa, Oklahoma. You fly in all the way from California to meet. Taylor is prepared to have dinner with you and is getting ready to whip out an engagement ring that you were not expecting. You did not feel that strongly about Taylor and did not want to hurt his feelings, so you simply held onto the ring, so you didn't say "yes" to him either. Instead, you told him, "let me think about it first." The moment has been perfectly captured in your mind. You remember the restaurant, the red wine, the bread, the salad with balsamic vinaigrette, and the chicken parmigiana, which tasted exquisite. Then, you boarded a plane bound for San Francisco, and you thought to yourself, "Jeez, I have no idea what to say. I feel like I'm a terrible person. Why did I ever do this to myself? I thought I loved Taylor, but I feel this cold place in my heart that I cannot explain. I just cannot marry him. It's not possible." You got really emotional on the plane ride back, recalling each moment of that dinner with him and the image of your boyfriend giving you the ring continuously looped in your mind. When you arrived in California, you called him and told him, "We're finished. I'm sorry, Taylor. I didn't tell you before, but we cannot keep going on like this. I don't mean to hurt you, but I cannot marry you. You're not the right person for me." You cried for about a week after that, constantly remembering that moment with your now ex-boyfriend.

This memory was graphic, because you remembered all the sights, smells, and tastes of the experience. It was easy for you to continuously go back to the memory, because it was an authentic moment. You felt a bit traumatized by it, because you couldn't believe what was happening. The proposal of your ex-boyfriend was so overwhelming that it became permanently embedded in your memory. You will not be the same person again. Through your five senses, you're able to remember exactly what had happened that day and are able to go back to this memory at any time.

Why Sensory Memory Works

We can recreate an emotion using our past experience and

then express it in an authentic way. When we use the five senses, we can give ourselves the complete picture of the experience. It can also help us access an emotional release object. This could be the sound of a clock, the smell of cigarettes in a home, or the sight of a sunset. For every memory, there is a subconscious sensory object that unlocks all the other parts of the memory. Once you have accessed the sensory object, then every detail from that moment comes flooding back into your mind.

Sensory memory enables us to remember past experiences, but it can also be traumatic, because if we get too lost in the memory, then we lose ourselves in it. If the memory takes over in our minds, it might be better to rely on a less potent resource, our imagination.

As soon as you have gone through the five senses and found something to emotionally connect to in your memory, then your recollection of the particular moment will come back to you easily and without much hesitation.

How to Use Your Sensory Memory

As you train your memory to remember experiences, think of it as an exercise that allows you release an emotion whenever you want. It can help you think like an actor and get out the feelings, because you know how to access your emotional release object. Let's now do some exercises to help you do that.

Sit in an armless chair and try to tense up your body and then let it loosen up, so that you look like a corpse that is draped on the chair. If you feel any stress, then try yelling out loud.

The moment you feel relaxed, think about your chosen memory. Go through every sense, one at a time. Continue going through the memory and try to find the emotion you felt. Take your time, because it may be a lengthy process. Once you've discovered the emotion, allow it to come over you so that you can remember every part of the emotional reaction.

To train yourself, it is important that you integrate regular practice throughout your day. Try to do this every day. When you have mastered your sensory memory, you will be able to bring up any emotion at any given moment. Then, you can get rid of the awkwardness of creating drama during everyday life, or if you're an actor, for an audition. If you can empathize with others, then you will likely be a good candidate to get more high profile roles and grow your network.

Why This Technique is For Actors and Everyone

This technique is useful for actors, because it allows them to produce the emotional responses on command, whenever they are doing a shoot or screening. However, you may be wondering, "how is this information useful for me if I'm not an actor?" Using sensory and affective memory will help you to relate to other's emotions. Whenever you can bring back the memories from the past, you become a better empath, who can identify with the struggles of people going through hard times. For example, when you see that a friend is going through the loss of a grandparent, you can recall the time when you lost your grandparent and how it felt to have your mother crying on your shoulder during that time. It is a vivid memory that does not go away, but allows you to put yourself in the place of another person, who is going through a similar experience.

On a more positive note, using sensory and affective memory helps you to feel the emotions of someone, who is experiencing a victory in their life. Whenever you hear about one of your friends, who has graduated summa cum laude from his university, you can remember the day you got a straight A award in school, and that made you feel awesome. When you have seen victory in your life, then you can celebrate others' successes also. It helps you to relate to others.

Case Study

Tom was a born-to-be actor. He was enrolled in a drama class at his school and he frequently starred in musicals for the theatre club. What made Tom a great actor was not only his ability to express himself, it was also his ability to recollect experiences from his past, and evoke the powerful emotions as he was acting on stage. For example, when he was playing Tony from West Side Story, he recalled the time when he fell in love with a girl for the first time and went on a date with her. This helped him to sing, "Maria" from the musical with more energy and affection than ever before, because he could empathize with the character, and he could sing his heart out, having had the experience of falling in love. That is something that people have to go through, including the sensations of break-ups whenever they happen. Re-creating those emotions is one of the biggest jobs for any actor.

Conclusion

To conclude, using the senses is going to be one of the best ways to remember events with clear detail. You will never be able to forget the sights and sounds of the various memories of your life. They will not vividly come to you on command without your active will power. They will come about with the sensory objects that enable you to remember everything. Within a moment, it all comes back to you. Every sensation and feeling is evoked all at once. To have a photographic memory, we recommend that you give this step a try, because you will remember things a lot better and make permanent the things of the past that have deeply affected you.

Step 7: Use Techniques that Increase Cognitive Activity and Add to Your Memory

In this chapter, we are going to go into the techniques that you can use to develop your brain's power to retain essential information. We will explain the methods that are used to increase cognitive activity. Allow your mind to soak in this vital information which will help you in your life.

1. Physical Activity: Working Out

In December 2013, researchers at the Boston University School of Medicine found out that physical activity provides health benefits for the brain and cognition. The 2013 study found that hormones that are released during exercise can aid in improving a person's memory. Researchers found similarities between hormone levels and a person's level of aerobic fitness, which was connected to a person's overall fitness level. In October 2013, researchers at Harvard Medical School conducted a study that linked exercise to overall brain activity . Exercise will enable you to do amazing things and to get the desired results you want for your mind. Exercise can increase your overall cognition, which aids in overall memory and retention of information. This has also been proven in children in their abilities in school. Exercise will significantly increase a person's ability to think clearly and reasonably (Bergland, 2014).

You may be thinking, "why should I go to the gym? What is that going to do to my memory?" Well, hear me out on this: exercise is going to boost your memory in different ways. For one, it is a kinesthetic activity that triggers muscle memory and other things that allow you to remember various aspects of your life. The more activities you do, the more your brain must engage in the exercise. Moreover, the exercise is useful both for the mind and for the body, because you're using a full-body workout. And the more you exercise, the better results you will see in this area.

But the thing is, you should not merely limit going to the gym as the only thing that you can do. The truth is, there are so many options available to you, as to what kind of exercise you can do. You can walk down the street and get your workout for the day. Better yet, use your phone as a pedometer and see how much you can walk each day. An average day can be about 10,000 steps, and once you've reached that threshold, you're doing well. But how you use those steps is up to you. However, if you can make an effort to do at least 10,000 steps a day, then you're set. You will see results, regardless of whether you choose to run, walk, or do some other aerobic exercises. Any which way you do it, you can benefit from the extra activity. Our bodies can transport us to numerous places, so we should use them to get us places. Don't only run for your car and make that your go-to transporter. Use your legs and feet; you were meant for movement, so do it!

Case Study

Most days, Tim was a couch potato. He preferred spending

time playing World of Warcraft on his computer, and he was unable to sleep at night because he stayed up until 4 am on his device. He was a bit addicted to say the least. Additionally, he was growing to be the irresponsible Joe in his house, because he lived with his parents. He had already graduated from college and had to pay his student loans. But he was unemployed. He couldn't get a job in his field of mass communications, although he had studied hard for it. He had $30,000 in student loan debt that he was slowly repaying on the minimum plan, but he felt that his life was hitting a stall. Tim's weight was also increasing each day. He had grown to be obese, and he frequently visited the doctor. The doctor told him, "Tim, you need to get your diet under control. You're 28 years old. I also want you to get some exercise. Work out! That's what you need to do." Feeling hit hard by these words, Tim realized he had to shape up as soon as he could. He needed to make some changes to his life fast because he was becoming obese, and he was feeling really low about himself. His self-esteem had hit rock bottom. He thought to himself, "What am I doing with my life? I wish I could get out of this."

One day, Tim went to the gym. It was his first time in over six years at a gym. He met a few other men, who were struggling with their weight, who were working out hard and were encouraging him. Tim said, "I'm looking to lose some pounds because I am overweight. Do you know of any ways I can do that?" Jason, who worked at the gym, told him, "Sure, bro. You can do it here. We can give you a plan for how you can get on the right track. Want to sign up today?" He agreed to do it, and within six months, he was able to get down to a healthy weight. Tim lost 20 pounds, and he felt great about his body. In the end, he was able to lower his weight, and he felt better.

2. Be Open to New Experiences

A study from October 2013 discovered that learning new and demanding skills is an essential way of increasing memory (Bergland, 2014). Less mentally strenuous activities such as listening to classical music or doing word searches and crossword puzzles are not going to provide the important benefits that you need. What you need to improve your memory and overall cognitive function is to be open to new experiences. When you do things that are outside of your comfort zone, you can do all the things you set your mind to, and it is incredible. Getting outside of your little box, where you might feel super comfortable, is an essential step to growth and maturity, not only in terms of your personal life but also for your mental life. We need to experience challenges; it's the only way we can go forward.

Challenging your brain is one of the most important things you can do for yourself. You need to give your brain ways to think deeper about certain things. Changing up your routine and taking a different route home is one way you can challenge your mind to think differently. Change is something that your brain needs in order to rework how you may do certain things. As creatures of habit, we often want to do things the same way we are used to. Whether or not we realize this, we're always doing this. We might be mindlessly doing the rat-race of life, only noticing one small detail as we look up from our phone on the subway or in the car.

Change is going to help develop your brain more. Have you been sitting in the same job for years now? Don't you want to change things up a bit? Do you feel too comfortable with what you do? Then, you should open up your mind to receive new experiences. This will do a lot to boost your overall cognition and ability to think and reason well. Changing jobs or cities will be helpful in getting you to where you want to be, not just because you want to be in a different position, but also because you want to have a different mentality, and this can only be done through changes in your life that make a difference in how you do things. Your brain will think more clearly, and you can come to solutions to new problems that you might have to confront along the way. By using your skills of creativity, you can truly find ways that will open your mind to new possibilities.

Case Study

Victoria was living a normal life as a millennial. She graduated from college in 2011 with a degree in nursing. Afterward, she spent three years in the healthcare industry, but she found it was draining, life-sucking, and super stressful, so she felt she needed to get out of it. She discovered that her life was stagnating, and it was difficult to function. Let me add, Victoria had lived in the same city her whole life, so she had no experiences of other places because she had not picked up and moved to other locations, or traveled very much. Therefore, she was feeling stagnant. Victoria had all her friends; her social life was thriving. And she had a great community with her ESL teaching work that she was doing on the side. Aside from that, things were pretty comfortable. One day, Victoria said to herself, "You know what, I need to do something daring and adventurous. I don't know what I'm doing with my life. I need to get out and experience the world!" So, Victoria searched online for different programs where she could teach English in China. She had never been to China and did not speak the language, but she knew in her heart, "I have to go!" Moreover, she signed up for the ESL job board and did a dozen of interviews for the right position. She landed a position at a university in Shanghai for a fall semester start.

In August, she boarded a plane and flew off to China. It was a new world of experiences for her. She felt that she was stepping outside of her comfort zone. It was making a big difference to her overall life. Her memory and cognition were enhanced, because she was taking in all the sights, sounds, smells, and tastes of a new place. It was overwhelmingly beautiful and scary at the same time. But Victoria knew that it was worth it to take this risk and venture to teach English where she did not know the language. Victoria struggled a bit at the beginning. She felt homesick and couldn't speak the language with anyone. She was the only one that could speak English in her community. But she felt invigorated by the wealth of new experiences, which were creating a visual memory that she would carry with her for the rest of her life.

3. Utilize Your Artistic and Creative Skills

Next, you need to utilize your artistic and creative skills that will help your overall cognition and memory. Often, we remember a song or piece of music and can instantly recall what it was like. Well, our musical ability can enhance our memory, as well, because we can do the things that will enable us to have better and more efficient cognition. Think about it. Many people are playing musical instruments these days, and it helps a lot with thinking clearly about other things in life. Musical training improves our overall cognition in profound ways because it will enable our minds to expand and grow.

Playing a musical instrument influences how the brain can interpret and take in various sensory information, especially in children who are below the age of seven. In a 2013 study, neuroscientists demonstrated how musical training promotes brain development and growth in young people (Bergland, 2014).

Case Study

Jamie loved classical music. He had studied it since he was a little boy. Jamie knew all the famous composers and could cite the classical music he heard on a given day in any cafe. He was an incredibly talented young man, but during his childhood, he struggled with memory development. He had developed epilepsy from a young age and would have seizures that would cause him to shake uncontrollably. He underwent an MRI scan when he was about nine years old, and it was at that time that the doctors determined he was suffering from epilepsy and quickly found a cure for it: musical treatment.

Furthermore, Jamie started taking violin lessons at age 9, which he thought would enhance his memory. He took violin with his teacher, Dr. Emily Carter, who helped him build courage and stamina to be a better violinist. Over time, Jamie learned the Suzuki method, which enables you to study musical pieces and memorize every movement from books 1-6.

Because Jamie played the violin, his muscle memory was enhanced. The violin is an enjoyable kinesthetic-type activity that involves motion, cognition, and emotion all at the same time. It is a fantastic form of exercise. He practiced over and over again until he could play the passages that he had worked on. Eventually, Jamie was playing musical pieces at recitals by memory, because he had worked so hard, but also, the violin was enabling him to remember all the things he had learned. Playing the violin created memories that will follow him for the rest of his life. And to this day, he can still visualize and remember the pieces that he learned, because they were all stored in his permanent long-term memory bank.

4. Social Connections

A February 2014 study found that there are consequences in being lonely for a while (Bergland, 2014). Loneliness can lead to psychological and cognitive decline, which can cause many different health problems. Therefore, it is crucial that you find ways to connect to other people. This will improve your overall mental health and cognitive health. Feeling isolated from others can lead to a host of problems, including sleep disruption, higher blood pressure, stress, and depression. Overall, if you are feeling lonely, then it is likely that you are not enjoying your life and you better get out of that funk as soon as you can. Being lonely can have some of the adverse effects that smoking or drinking can have on your body. We are not meant to live in isolation from one another. Instead, we are meant to form long lasting connections with others. Therefore, it is crucial that we find ways to relate to others and build lasting relationships that can be an antidote to our loneliness.

Social connections are good for our brain because we think a lot when we talk to other people. We form lasting relationships with people because there is a visual aspect to it, which influences how we feel, think, and react in different situations. As we continue to talk to people and spend time with them, we enhance our overall memories, because we can enjoy the times we have with them, and we can remember the good times and forget about the bad times.

Case Study: Frank

Frank was a hard-core introvert. As a teenager, he never talked to other kids. He preferred to spend time alone rather than engage in meaningful relationships with his peers. He was painfully shy. He didn't want to admit to his weakness, because he had a secret pride in his abilities. But what Frank didn't realize was how deeply depressed he was. He didn't have any friends, and he was very lonely. People noticed that he was not eating and only drinking water day after day. He also was shying away from any social interactions. Then, one day, Peter came up to Frank and asked him, "Hey, Frank! How are you? Do you want to get together and have dinner and go watch a movie?" Frank was very nervous as he replied with "Yeeessss... hmm... sure, no problem. I'd love to." From that moment onward, Frank began a friendship with Peter. They would hang out every weekend. Frank still struggled with loneliness sometimes, because he thought that he couldn't engage with his peers. But as he grew in his friendship with Peter, he became more confident. Pretty soon, he could talk to his peers and invited them over to his house, where he would cook dinner for them. His first dinner party was the coming of age process for Frank, as he finally entered into the sphere of social life, and also benefited greatly from that time.

Throughout this time, Frank saw some noticeable improvement in his test scores. He started studying with his peers. They formed a study group and would go to the library on Wednesday nights to study. Because of this, Frank would spend lots of time with his friends. Together, they memorized all the chemistry formulas for their chemistry test. It was great teamwork! They had so much fun together; it was terrific. And then, it came time for final exams. Together, everyone crammed and studied very hard. Frank nailed the exam with a 95 (meaning an A). He was so happy, because he had memorized all the chemistry formulas, and he had done so with the help of his friends.

5. Mindfulness and Meditation

In a 2013 study at Harvard Beth Israel hospital, researchers were able to discover that brain changes that come with meditation and stress relief play in an essential role in preventing disorders such as Alzheimer's disease and dementia later in life (Bergland, 2014). Mindfulness can help you to combat all these things because it helps your memory to develop more over time.

Mindfulness is a practice in which you can focus on meditation and allowing yourself to remain poised in the present moment for a given time. With meditation, you rest in the current circumstance, knowing that you are mindful of your surroundings. It's a way to unwind and get out of the busyness of everyday life. Practicing mindfulness is one of the most important ways that you can improve your memory, as well, because you can remember a lot more when you are not stressed or filled with anxiety.

As you get out of your stress, you're able to experience increased freedom and autonomy to do what you like. Then, you don't have to think so much about your future. You're so focused on the here and now that you can concentrate a lot better, and you don't feel burdened over the weight of things in your life. It is vital that you find ways to practice mindfulness every day so you can achieve your life goals and say no to stress.

There has been a connection between stress and chronic mental disorder and decline, so if we can avoid more of that, the better off we will feel and be. It is crucial that we find ways to curtail our stress. Although it is an ever-present reality that we must face, we have to keep our guard up or else we fall into anxiety and despair, which can cause chronic mental impairment that can affect us for the rest of our life. Therefore, if you want to improve your memory and prevent mental decline later in life, it is better for you to fight off the stress now at this moment in your life.

Case Study

Kelly was chronically stressed. She always forgot her keys and sometimes her appointments. Her schedule was so busy that she became increasingly forgetful. Kelly was dying under the wave of stress that was infecting her whole being. She did not know what to do with herself. When she arrived at work, she would often experience sweating and panting (with shortness of breath). She was out of shape and overweight, as well. Additionally, she was fighting back feelings of low self-esteem. Because Kelly was struggling with her weight, she was also experiencing depressive episodes. She did not know what to do about her memory problem because of her frequent lapses. Moreover, she went to her doctor to see what he could do to help her. He recommended that she go and see a therapist who could take care of her situation. So, she went to see Dr. Fitzgerald, who was a counselor. The counselor immediately recommended that she do some guided meditation every day to increase her memory and to make her less stressed. Kelly then started to meditate for one hour every day. It was amazing. She could feel the results in her mind immediately. She practiced in her room every day, and she could see that things were getting better. Every day, she became more and more optimistic, seeing the light of day rise from the darkness. It was amazing. Then, pretty soon, Kelly started practicing mental exercises that were recommended by her doctor to increase her photographic memory. Soon after, she never forgot her appointments. She always remembered where she had put her keys. Pretty soon, she was no longer forgetful Kelly and became mindful Kelly, who was continuously aware of her present circumstances. At work, she grew to feel less stressed and calmer. She sometimes felt under pressure, but she still thought she was able to handle anything that was given to her because she grew in confidence and strength. It was a great testimony of her healing.

6. Decrease Anxiety and Stress

Finally, one of the most important things you can do for yourself to increase your memory is to reduce the stress that is in your life. Our stress affects our ability to function and to do things effectively. The more we are stressed, the more prone we are to getting sick and feeling generally unwell.

Now, granted, you cannot get rid of most stress in your life. We continually have to battle it in our lives. But what we can do is say "no" to stressful situations that are hurting us and causing us to roll over and feel miserable about ourselves. We need to find ways to get rid of the overall anxiety that permeates our current modern society. Too much of our world is ruled by chaos and disorder. The fear of the other, which is used in modern philosophy, causes us to think like Sartre in that "hell is other people," therefore, we want to become reclusive and hide our caves.

However, what we must do, is rid ourselves of the unnecessary stress that burdens our lives. Our lives are ruled by busyness so that we are unable to do all the things that we want to do. We pack our schedules to the brim with activities, events, work, among many other things. It is too bad that we are always experiencing the pain and anxiety of our life; however, it is not enough to keep going through it. So, we suffer and suffer some more.

What I would like to recommend to everyone who wants to improve their photographic memory is to stop. Stop! Hold your horses! Don't go any further. Our society demands us to "go! Go! Go!" But I want you to stop and hold that thought and take a deep breath. Hold it in and then exhale. Allow yourself to de-stress and detox. It's vital for your overall well-being. You have to be gentle with yourself and try to do things that will bring you greater happiness. Be kind to yourself and allow yourself to be filled with joy.

As you de-stress, you will realize that you are taking ownership over the present situation and you're able to breathe more easily. You won't be burdened by the difficulties and challenges of your life. Instead, you will be motivated and empowered to do great things. And your memory will become more precise than ever before because you won't have all that stress clouding your judgment. Finally, you will find that de-stressing will be the best step for you in your fight to save your memory from decline and cognitive dysfunction.

Case Study

Maria had panic attacks frequently. She was sitting on the edge every day. As a result, she was waiting for something bad to happen to her. She lived in fear of making mistakes most days. And sure enough, she started to make a ton of mistakes at her work, because she was binging on caffeine and not getting enough sleep at night. Her job was causing her a great deal of anxiety. Consequently, she was unable to remember most of the things on her agenda. Her short-term memory experienced lapses so that she was unable to use anything except her working memory, which expired every day. Fortunately, Maria was working on side projects that she thought could get everything going for her. But she soon realized her job was killing her. It was causing her so much stress and anxiety. She also didn't like her coworkers. They were negative and caused her a great deal of grief.

One day, Maria had an epiphany. She realized something and said to herself, "What am I doing with my life? It seems that everything is falling to pieces. I cannot keep doing this at my work. I need to pursue my dream, to open my own business. That's what I wanted to do before. I've already saved up enough money. Why don't I quit my job and start my business? It will help me a great deal. I will feel loads better and take that stress off my back." That's exactly what Maria did. She quit her job and opened up her own business. It was one of the scariest and most unforgettable experiences of her life, but Maria knew that it was going to greatly decrease her stress level, so she wouldn't have to worry about others and their opinions of her.

Opening her own business was a great decision for Maria, because she could think more clearly about her goals and she was less anxious for the future. Also, she had a better overall memory of things, which was a great plus. Because she no longer struggled with anxiety, she could do all the things that she planned to do without worrying. Pretty soon, her overall cognitive abilities were impacted in a positive way so that she could complete her assignments and work on her business in the comfort of her own home. Working from the home office enabled her to concentrate and get more things done, and she could have more flexible time to spend with herself. In the end, she was happy and felt that her memory was clearer than before.

7. Listen to Classical Music or Play an Instrument

One of the ways to increase our mind's ability to remember is by listening to music. The genre that seems to increase our brain's cognitive activity is classical music. So, if you are looking to find something to listen to, keep an ear out for Beethoven, Mozart, or Schumann. Allow yourself to soak in the sounds of the instruments, including the strings, brass, and percussion. Focus on the different sections of the musical piece, and you will be able to remember different parts. Classical music increases our mind's concentration so that we can complete the tasks that are in front of us. The more we fill our minds with positive thoughts and increased brain activity, the more we can think clearly about things. And that enables us to have a better memory that can remember details.

If we think about Gustav Holst's, "The Planets," we can imagine ourselves transported to another time, a bygone era. As we listen to "Jupiter," we experience teleportation to a zone where we are aware of the things around us and think of the rings of Jupiter and the excitement of outer space. Also, we hear a famous hymn in the middle, which reminds us of Old England. There are many images that we can have as we listen to Holst's "The Planets," which gives us an even brighter memory of things.

Whenever you listen to classical music, allow yourself to paint images of a scene or a concert in your mind's eye, and think about it. Then, when you listen to it again, you can imagine yourself in that situation. The effect of classical music will significantly enhance your imagination and memory so that you will be able to remember things.

Case Study

For years, Whitney played the violin. She spent years getting better at playing. Additionally, she went through the Suzuki Violin School, which enabled her to learn more effectively and memorize all the passages she had to play. Through memorizing the passages, her memory significantly increased, and she was able to imagine different things going on within that.

In her own time, Whitney listened to the "Four Seasons," and she memorized different passages from the "Spring" concerto. She continually listened to the music and had it cemented into her mind. After a while, she was able to play the piece from memory. She memorized it for an audition for Juilliard Music School. Whitney auditioned with the "Spring" concerto, and was accepted to the music school with a full-ride scholarship, so that she could attend tuition-free. It was a fantastic experience.

Conclusion

There are six main ways that you can allow your brain to function well and protect your memory against aging and mental decline. These will also be important to get you in the right place with your photographic memory. It is vital that you find ways of protecting yourself against all the things that can affect your brain. You have to give yourself challenges so you won't stay stagnant. No one wants to stay in the same place, so you absolutely must find ways of improving yourself and arriving at the destination that is going to benefit you the most. Always move forward and never look back. Allow yourself to move forward in the confidence that you can accomplish all that you set out to do. Create the memory and allow your brain to function to its full capacity by taking the advice in this chapter.

Step 8: Take Steps to Increase Mental Alertness

In this eighth step, we will talk about how you can take extra steps to increase your mental alertness and have more memory power to support your photographic memory (Alban, 2019).

To have a positive active mind, we need to increase our mental alertness, which enables us to be awake all the time. Often, we are sleepy, because we don't get enough sleep, or we feel groggy having slept too long. Some people cannot open their eyes in the morning, because they've had too much to drink the night before. In any case, it is essential that we find ways to increase our mental alertness, which declines as we age. When we become older, we lose the vital energy that we had in our youth and need more sleep to restore our systems. Let's now look at some ways we can increase our mental strength and stamina so we can endure whatever situation we are faced with.

1. Hydration

Because our bodies are mostly made up water, we need to continually feed it with fluids during the day. It is crucial that we provide it with enough water to maintain a state of equilibrium and to feel that we are at our most optimum level. If we don't drink enough water, we will become dehydrated, and this affects not only our physical body but also our cognitive ability to function. In fact, we can lose concentration when we're dehydrated and experience symptoms that mimic dementia. It can be very dangerous for your body when you don't drink enough. We can go for long periods without food, and it is not a problem. But we cannot survive more than three days without water. Therefore, we must stay hydrated at all times if we want to be in the right place. This is especially the case if we are exercising when we have to use about 10% of our body's fluids through the intensive workouts. Try your best to drink as much as possible.

I know that most people don't like to drink pure water because it is boring and does not provide a refreshing taste that most people like. Instead, it has no taste but feels fresh. If you don't want to drink too much water, then try a fruit juice, a sports drink, or tea instead. There are plenty of fluids that would qualify to replenish your body with needed fluid that you can consume each day. It does not necessarily have to be water. Although coffee can dehydrate, it can also be used as a fluid in your diet to help you, as you refresh yourself each day.

Case Study

Leo was a runner. He loved to go outside and run. But unfortunately, he did not consume enough water, so he experienced dehydration. One day, he nearly collapsed. He had red bruises that appeared on his skin in areas that were dehydrated. He almost had to go to the emergency room to replenish his body fluids. It was a frightening sight. Leo recognized after that incident that he had to replenish his body each day and drink more because otherwise, he would not be able to cognitively function. Leo also had trouble concentrating in school at the time, because he had not drunk enough water. Consequently, he could not study well and had terrible grades. After he started drinking more water, Leo felt that he could concentrate a lot better and his grades improved. It was a good result of hydration.

2. Watch the Caffeine

All of us may consume caffeine on a given day. It is a wonderful creation that we benefit from because it helps mitigate the effects of having a sleepless night. Most people in America love to down a couple of cups of coffee every morning. It has been proven that coffee can improve our cognitive performance, so if we drink more, we will see better results. Conversely, if we drink too much, we will experience more dehydration, feel sleepy, and crash in the middle of the day. Furthermore, it is vital that we are careful with how much caffeine we put in our bodies every day. It can cause problems with your sleep and make it harder to fall asleep at night.

Caffeine can also make us jittery and keep us up on our feet at night. Think about how much caffeine you might consume before a conference presentation. You may get so nervous that you start shaking and sweating. Caffeine can also cause shortness of breath, in which case we are unable to keep our concentration in high-performance situations. Therefore, you should stick to a bottle of water, so you won't be shaky and won't be running to the bathroom every five minutes (Alban, 2019).

Additionally, the cognitive effects of caffeine wear off over time, which causes you to crash mid-day. Consequently, you cannot concentrate and feel the need to take a long nap to feel better. Sleeping will be one of the most important things you can do for your memory to feel at your best.

Case Study

On a given day, Sharon would drink 5-8 cups of coffee. She would go to Starbucks at least three times a day and fill up on more coffee throughout the day at the office. She was a "coffee-holic." She would say, "wake up and smell the coffee, people! It's a brand new day! I'm ready to take on the world!" Sharon was able to get a lot done at work, because she was continually downing her cup of coffee, and it was clear that she was doing a lot. But inwardly, she was always trembling, because she had not gotten enough sleep the night before. Her addiction was getting the best of her because she would collapse at home after each day of work. The caffeine was wearing off and causing her to drift off into a deep slumber. And then she would awake from her nap and be wide awake until 3 am. This continued on and off for the longest time. At first, it wasn't causing any problems, but pretty soon, it was making her late for work, because she hit snooze on her alarm and woke up late, and she was getting sick, because her system was in overdrive, yet she could not stop. Eventually, her body could not take it anymore.

After getting sick, Sharon went to see her doctor, who told her that she needed to stop drinking caffeine for two months. He wanted to wean her body off all that caffeine that was controlling her mind and body. He told Sharon, "I think the caffeine has been taking over, and it's no longer you talking, but the caffeine. You must watch out next time and not overdo it. This will also help your memory to be at its best." So, Sharon tried. The regimen was exhausting for her. Every day was a struggle that she had to fight, but she overcame it. Then, after two months, she was able to put herself back on coffee, and limit herself to only two cups a day. In the end, she was able to restore her concentration and productivity at work.

3. Lose the GPS and Find Other Ways to Get Home

Because we have a GPS system on our mobile devices, we have become lazier because all we have to do is search for our destination on our devices and it will guide us to our destination. Granted, this has made it easier for us to go anywhere in the world. We become less likely to get lost because we use the navigation system on our phone to help us go places. At the same time, we have lost our sense of a personal human compass, which can determine in which direction to go. Gone are the days where we would rely on a map to get us anywhere. There's no need to memorize anything because all the information is freely available to us through the Internet. However, with this constant reliance on GPS technology, our minds are becoming duller and less likely to remember things. Our spatial-visual memory becomes impaired, and it can lead to our brain's shrinkage, as a result of not using the powers of the imagination that are responsible for helping us remember where things are (Alban, 2019).

If you want to improve your memory, turn off the GPS, and

try looking at a map or signs on the road to determine how to get to your destination. Try to find an alternative way to get home from an unfamiliar place. If you do this, you will do amazing things for your brain, because you will be using cognitive powers of concentration that focus intently on the different markers that your mind has carved out to navigate where your destination is. It is very healthy for you. So, help your brain and turn it off.

Case Study

Mark loved roadtrips with his friends. Many times, he would go across the country to get to know different sights and destinations. One summer, he and his buddies drove from Cleveland, Ohio to Seattle, Washington. It took about 36 hours to make the entire trip with stops along the way and a few overnight stays in hotels. But Mark had one weakness. He had a hard time with navigation. As a result, he couldn't read maps and had to rely a lot on his GPS to get him where he needed to be. Instead of enjoying the scenery of where he was going on these road trips, he focused on his GPS the entire time.

Mark's buddies told him, "Dude! You need to ditch the GPS. It's not helping you drive more effectively. You're just staring at the GPS. Why don't you use a map or look at the signs?" Mark decided to listen to their advice stubbornly, and he got rid of his GPS. At first, he struggled to find his way to places, because he had become dependent on the technology to get him everywhere. But pretty soon, Mark was using his brain instead of technology. He recognized that he could come up with creative solutions to his problems rather than trusting that the GPS could do everything for him. In the end, he got to the places where he needed to be.

To this day, Mark does not use a GPS. Instead, he memorizes a map and makes a memory palace in his mind, which enables him to recall details while he is driving. He uses visuals such as signs on the road to help him arrive to his destination. It has made an enormous difference in his life.

4. Pursue a Hobby

In addition to losing the GPS, you should pursue something that gives you joy and passion. Find something that drives you. What is it that gets you up in the morning and keeps you going in life? Find something that you can keep doing for an extended period. Socializing can be included in that. Maybe you like to paint. Join a painting class. Or, perhaps, you wish to sing. Join a choir. Perhaps, you enjoy reading and writing, so you could try joining a book club or a writer's club. Do things that will help you get better at what you want to do with your life (Alban, 2019).

Finding your passion is going to help you with your memory, as well, because when you love what you do, you will remember things a lot more easily. If you're doing things that don't interest you or don't give you joy, you'll think to yourself, "Well, forget about that. It's total trash." Doing the same old job that brings no benefits, except a paycheck, can drain the energy from you and suck you dry. Therefore, it is vital that you find ways to get out your creative juices and do things that will make you happier.

Case Study

Annelies worked in a tourism organization in Paris. She loved to ride her bike to work, which was something that many Dutch people did in the Netherlands. Annelies was very fond of travel and enjoyed visiting new places and meeting new people. Annelies loves new experiences and taking risks. She had traveled to almost all countries in Europe. Her goal was to visit all of them by 2020, so she is currently working on this goal. She still hasn't visited the Baltic states, which are often under visited by many people. Although she is single and doesn't have a boyfriend, she loves to socialize with others and will sometimes go to the expat bars.

What has given her a collective memory of her experience is the travel that she has done over the years. Living abroad as an expat has given her a place to live that is filled with adventure. No two days are the same. Annelies is always learning and growing. Being a resident of another country is hard, especially for a person who is going at it solo, so that makes her a brave woman. She has endured many hardships the past couple years, having lost her boyfriend to cancer and her parents' divorce. But Annelies remains strong and grounded. She will not waver with the wind when times get hard. She knows that she has been through tough times, but she can get through everything that life throws at her because she is resilient and hardworking.

Annelies is very sharp and remembers vivid details. Having traveled and spoken foreign languages, she thinks a lot and her brain is constantly working, which enables her to sharpen her skills. It also helps with her fine motor skills. This helps her to ride her bike effectively and watch out for the vehicles on the road.

Annelies has developed her passion for travel. Her hobby has brought her many places. She is delighted with her life because she has discovered new places and people, and it has helped her to remember all the experiences she has had. Although her memory is not perfect, she can still remember many things, and that helps her to live a meaningful life, full of lasting relationships. Her life is filled with a beautiful edifice of knowledge and education that will last a lifetime.

Step 9: Study Skills: What You Can Work On Now to Increase Your Photographic Memory

In this chapter, we are going to discuss several different study skills you can apply to your life so you can increase your photographic memory (Leyden, 2019). These techniques will help you as you are studying for a test, doing school work, or completing various tasks requiring the use of your brain. Let's dive in.

1. Spaced Repetition

Most people know that rote memorization is not the way to study for your next test. Many people try to memorize words on a page by merely staring down at the paper and then five minutes later, they are unable to recall what they have already learned. Instead of solely relying on rote memorization to get us where we need to be, there are other ways that enable students to remember the things they need to know. One of these ways is spaced repetition.

Spaced repetition requires that the student continuously study vocabulary and other content for an extended period using flashcards, apps, and other tools to help with studying. Spaced repetition helps the student to review the material they learned in class and follow up each lesson. People use this method all the time as they review words when memorizing. It is a useful method because you can update your knowledge and keep studying until you remember what you have learned in class. Spaced repetition is done so that you're able to recognize the vocabulary step-by-step and not all at once, as is common with cramming.

Why is cramming harmful to your brain? Korean teenagers are notorious for studying and memorizing material that is given in front of them. They study, study, study, and then they take the test, and immediately once it's done, they forget everything that they learned. It's almost as if they learned nothing in the process. It is sad that many people forget all the things that they had learned after the test as if they never learned the material in the first place. Think of the people who study for the GRE, TOEFL, SAT, or other standardized tests and after the test they forget hundreds or even thousands of words they "acquired" in their cramming sessions. Unfortunately, that is the case for many people in the United States, as well.

Rather than cramming down all that information into your brain, it is helpful to space things out a bit, so you can manage how you study and do a little bit every night. Our minds can only consolidate so much information at a time before they become overloaded with information. As a result, it cannot pack information within too short of a time. Our short-term memory can only retain a certain amount of data before it is not possible to hold it in anymore. Therefore, it is vital that you give yourself a break sometimes, to offset the information overload that we always experience when we're stressed.

Case Study

Adam was studying for the GRE, and he bought a review book that enabled him to look at all the materials that he needed to look over. He realized that his mathematical concepts were lacking and that he needed to make up for it by memorizing different formulas and problems. Adam had heard about spaced repetition from a workshop at his school, where he was able to get some ideas to enhance his study skills. He studied for three months for the GRE, and every day, he would practice math problems that would be on the GRE. He looked at geometry problems for one week, and he would practice solving them every day. Then, he would go online and take tests, which were instantly graded, so he could get feedback immediately. He used flashcards and apps to help him remember key concepts that he was using to solve the problems. Although it was difficult for him, he was still able to solve all the problems every day. Additionally, he hired a tutor to help him fill in the gaps of his knowledge. His tutor helped him practice frequently so that he could get more feedback and further assistance in studying for the test. After three months, Adam felt more confident, because he could remember the mathematical topics he had studied with ease. They were ingrained, not only in his working memory, but also in his permanent memory, so it was an effective way of studying for the test. Adam used a variety of methods to remember words and formulas. When he got to the test, he was able to effortlessly solve the problems within the given time, and aced the exam.

2. Use Your Smartphone Apps Including Study Blue and Memrise

The second thing you should do is use apps on your smartphones, such as Study Blue and Memrise. These apps allow a person to use spaced repetition technology to study at any time and in any place, wherever there is Internet. You can download the apps on your smartphone or computer. The apps are particularly useful if you are a teacher and want to use technology in your class. For many courses, professors and teachers can use spaced repetition technology to create memorization games, in which individual students and groups can practice memorizing vocabulary. Using apps like Study Blue, students can have fun getting to know the different words that they acquire over time.

Study Blue and Memrise can also be shared with an entire class. The teacher or professor can make a list of words and then share it with the whole class through their smartphones, so the students could study at home and do all the memorizing in the comfort of their bedrooms. It will help the students to cement the information in their minds, as they practice spaced repetition on their devices.

Case Study

William had difficulty memorizing information. He was not good at rote memorization because when he took vocabulary tests during his English class, he would always fail. He wanted to study right before, but immediately upon looking at a paper, he forgot the information presented, as if he had never looked at the words. William talked to his English teacher about coming up with ways to boost his vocabulary and perform well on tests. His teacher, Mr. Kyle, told him that he needed to use spaced repetition exercises to get better at memorizing vocabulary. So, Kyle invited him to Studyblue to the deck of cards that were being used in class. Mr. Kyle realized that students like William needed self-study tools at home, so he made them available to all students and gave them out freely. It helped a lot with the confidence of the students. They took off with it and had a great time studying. The whole class was scoring above 90% on the vocabulary quizzes because they were getting enough practice while studying at home.

3. For Language Classes, Take Vocab Tests Online for Self-Study

Usually, you will find that many people study vocabulary in foreign language classes, where it's necessary to memorize a lot of words. Vocabulary needs to be continuously assessed in the classroom to ensure that students are correctly learning the texts they are studying. Doing so online is a great way to get students to study hard because they can check their progress and see their results immediately. Finding the right online resources will enable your class to perform well in no time.

In addition to the online tests, you should try to use the words or concepts from your lists in a sentence or in a specific context to cement everything in your mind. It is not enough to merely rely on your memorization of the word without some background. You will quickly forget it if you don't use it in a sentence. Therefore, it is crucial that you find ways to integrate the vocabulary study in practical ways so that you can see it in action all the time.

Case Study

Joyce had a hard time remembering all the vocabulary content she had acquired in her French class, so she wanted to find a way to remember it better. She knew that cramming was not the way to go, but she was struggling to find something that could work for her. She asked her teacher to help her figure out a way to improve her vocabulary. The teacher told her to go online and find vocabulary quizzes that she could design herself and solve. Joyce went online and discovered a way that she could prepare a vocabulary test and then take it afterwards. This helped her a lot. She also improved in her overall performance in class; so, it was a success.

4. Draw Images of Stories and The Concepts that You are Studying

One thing that you might think is childish is drawing a picture of the various stories and concepts that we study in school. In elementary school, we probably did this often. However, when we draw a picture, we can have a glimpse into our imaginations. When we imagine what we learn, then we can remember things a lot better. Don't feel ashamed if you enjoy drawing pictures. Do it for your memory! You can remember the stories that you learn about in literature class if you put a storyboard together. It will help you visualize everything. And then, maybe one month, one year, or three years later, you will have the memory of that image for the rest of your life. That doesn't happen the same way every time, but it could prove to be helpful to your overall memory.

Case Study

An artist by trade, Colleen loved to draw pictures. In school, she would get bored easily so she would often draw in her notebook. Sometimes, she would make doodles of her teacher. Other times, she would draw the different experiences in her life. She was skilled at this, and she always loved to draw unique images of the various things she was studying. When it came time to do group work, Colleen always wanted to sit by herself and draw on her own. She was quite introverted, so individual work was never a problem for her. One day her teacher told her, "Colleen, I want you to share your pictures with your friends. They can interpret your picture and see if it corresponds with what we're reading. How does that sound?" Colleen replied: "Ok, I will do what the teacher says." Colleen never regretted that moment after she started talking to her friends. She immediately felt thrilled by it. Her friends started listening to what she said about the stories in the class. She described every detail of the story, just as she had drawn it, which matched up with what the students had been reading. It was awesome. Colleen was proud of herself. She knew that she had great ideas to share about the texts the class was looking at, and she wanted to share them with the others. This made her grow as a student, and she also helped other students as well.

5. Recite a Text for Poetry Slams and Other Competitions

To train your memory like a pro, make memorizing into something you can enjoy with competitions, such as poetry slams and memorizing contests. Recitation can be a fun way to memorize with your class, group of friends, or another circle. Better yet, you can provide some prize or incentive to make it more motivating and less dreadful of an experience for everyone.

When you read something out loud, it engages your heart and mind into the text that you are reading. You can navigate memorizing even better when you know the book by heart. Remembering both the written and spoken version of the text is going to help your memory a lot so that you can share your ideas with others. It is going to give you so much more confidence to achieve your goals. Furthermore, we urge you to try out this technique as you are memorizing a script or poem. It will help you be more assertive and apt to take on any challenge that comes your way.

6. Use a Memory Peg to Remember Things By What They Rhyme With

If you want to get better at memorizing things for a test, try making each word rhyme with a number. You can assign these numbers as a sort of secret code you can work with daily. Let's look at some examples.

1 = son

2 = through

3 = see

4 = more

5 = thrive

6 = sticks

7 = Kevin

8 = state

9 = fine

10 = when

But how would you make connections when making a grocery list, for example? If you were creating a list to go to the store but forgot it, how would you be able to remember? Think of ways to link together your list using images like these:

Eggs: Imagine the sunrise over a snowy place or eggs that are being cooked sunny side up.

Onions: Think about animals having a war with each other and using onion grenades.

Carrot: Imagine a rifle shooting out carrot bullets.

Bacon: Think about bacon fruits on a tree.

By visualizing the images on your list, then you can remember what you thought you had forgotten. Use these links to retain as much information as possible.

7. Slow Down the Studying

When you're studying for different tests, it is best to slow down as much as possible and learn fewer things. You may be tempted to try to memorize as many words as possible at a given time, but studies have shown that less is more when it comes to studying. When you can review and learn more in that short period, it will help you in your overall retention. Who wants to study so much when they can study just a little bit at a time. Then, they can remember everything. Let's look at a case study of this technique.

Case Study

Kane always thought he had to study hard to get into university. He used to cram for every exam. He failed five times out of 10 because he could not review the material and retain it. His brain couldn't handle the memorization of the content. He didn't realize that he had to do a little bit each day to make it stick. Kane hired a tutor to help him with memorizing information. The tutor gave him everything he needed to know about it. Kane then started taking 10 words each day and using various study techniques to help him memorize for his tests. Then, he added a few more words each day. Bit by bit, he learned the content. By the time he had to take the test, he knew everything, and started getting 100% on all assignments. It was fantastic, all due to his tutor, who had faithfully helped him.

8. Watch a documentary on the topic that you're studying.

One excellent way of learning about something is to watch a documentary on the topic. Documentaries will enable you to see the entire story if the question is about history. Then, you can remember the key details from the story, and you will be able to see the actual re-enactment of it. This technique is especially helpful for students who can't visualize situations by themselves. When you can rely on the imagination of someone else, then you can get a better picture of the things that you study. When in doubt, or when you are struggling to form a mental image of what you're studying, hop onto Youtube and watch a documentary about it. It can give you more motivation to study harder and more effectively. Then, you can ace that test. You can improve your memory this way.

9. Take Study Breaks

When you are studying, remember that you need to give yourself breaks, because you won't be able to retain the information that you are reading up on after studying it for 1 hour 30 minutes. Therefore, it is crucial that you give yourself a break after 45-50 minutes. Do yourself a favor, take a coffee break, and get away from work for a while. It will clear your head and make you feel more refreshed and ready to conquer more than ever. Do it for your memory's sake.

Case Study: Tracy

Tracy was an intense student. She studied hard at the library. Sometimes, she couldn't stop reviewing for different classes. In a way, she was addicted to her studies, and it was because she was passionate about the topic. But often, she would study for 10 hours straight without any breaks in between. Soon after that, she started to experience fatigue, which caused her to fall asleep during class. Her mental alertness was not readily there; she had to change. Her mentor recommended that she take more breaks and go outside to play with her friends. Tracy realized she was studying too hard, so she tried segmenting her time, so that she could find periods of rest with times of intensive studying. Knowing that you can only concentrate on something for about 30 minutes at a time, Tracy started to take breaks after every hour. She would go to the bathroom, get a drink of water, or walk down the hallway of her library, so she could get her blood flowing.

After taking breaks, Tracy noticed that not only could she study better, she could also remember what she was reviewing much better. The scheduled pauses gave her time to relax and experience more freedom. Tracy was able to get back her concentration, so she could study more. Gradually, Tracy also developed a work-life balance, which allowed her to live a healthier lifestyle.

10. Find New Study Spaces

Often, when we study or do work, we think that staying in the same comfortable place is where we can get the most done.

However, information retention can improve when you change up the location of where you are studying from time to time. Most of the time, students like to study at home or in the library, but finding new study spaces can help your brain to adjust to new situations and learn new material more quickly and easily. This helps you to experience new developments in your studying. You may think that finding that perfect spot to study is the main thing that you're after. However, what you should realize is that your brain is meant to have a break from familiar places, and you should play along with that. Giving your mind a pause from every day can enhance your overall memory and ability to retain the given material that you are studying.

Case Study

Dexter was continually searching for the best place to study, but he wanted to stay in the same area every time. Unfortunately, he realized that he was stagnating every time he would find a good place to study. Then, he would feel like he couldn't study there anymore. As a result, he had a hard time concentrating on his work. Dexter wasn't a bright student. He had decent grades, but he never received A's on his assignments. Soon, he felt as if his academic life was becoming more stale and less interesting. After talking to his friends, Dexter realized that he had to change it up. He couldn't simply stay in the same study space every time. He had to get up and move to a new place. Sometimes, he could study in a cafe or library, and at times, he could simply stay in his dorm room and chill out with Maroon 5 music playing in the background. Dexter noticed that studying became more intriguing each time he did this, because he could adapt his mind to a new study place, and it affected his overall memory retention of the concepts he was studying. So, Dexter dedicated his time to changing his study environment every week. He would visit at least three different places. After completing this experiment, Dexter noticed that he remembered a lot more the details of his assignments and things he had to memorize. His grades went up, and it was a success, thanks to his dedication and hard work.

11. Never Pull An All-Nighter. Ever.

It has been proven that all-nighters are one of the worst things that you can do for your body and mind ("How Bad is Pulling an All-Nighter," n.d.). In college, it is common to pull an all-nighter before final exams, with last-minute cramming. However, the thing is, if you do this, you will likely put everything into your temporary mindset and then forget everything the day of the test. But also, as we have shown, sleep is essential for your memory, and if you lose sleep the night before a big test, then you will likely not remember anything and potentially fail big time. Then again, there are exceptions to this rule. Some students are masters at all-nighters and can stay up all night for a whole week and then sleep the next week. This is an abominable practice. Therefore, you should try to steer away from this option, because it is not going to help you learn anything. It will make you forget so many things. And your body will not thank you. It will implore you to give it sleep. Advice from the expert: do not ever pull an all-nighter. It is never a good idea. Sleep is always the best policy. Party hearty is for first-year students in their first semester of college. For a grad student or working professional, that is never an option.

Furthermore, my best advice is to grow up and stop doing things that are juvenile and that will not help you in the long run.

Case Study

Daniel K. was an engineering student at a no-name school in Tennessee. He lived with a humanities student. Daniel was very messy and sloppy, and his roommate was orderly and kept his stuff organized. Daniel tended to be a very disorganized student, yet he was able to get decent grades in his engineering classes. During the final exam season, he would pull all-nighters all the time. This annoyed his roommate, who was trying to sleep. Daniel did not realize until later that this practice was futile and was getting him nowhere. He continued to binge on caffeine and sometimes drank coffee until 5 am. Additionally, he did not take a shower and smelled quite rancid at times, due to his lack of hygiene. His roommate, Jason, said, "Daniel, why don't you go to bed? I'm going to bed. So, I suggest you do it too. I'm sure that you don't need to stay up all night studying for this exam. So, why not get some shut-eye now and see what happens?" Daniel replied to Jason: "That's an idea. I'll try it and see what becomes of it." Daniel stopped studying and realized the importance of sleep. He gradually improved in his ability to study, and his grades went up. It was a success story, proven by Jason's tried and tested ways. In the end, Daniel was able to finish strong in college.

Conclusion

Study skills will be useful to help you get to where you want to be with your photographic memory. Training your mind each day to study for various things that you may be learning will enable you to remember things with more clarity than ever before. You will recall accurately and effectively all the things you study, because you have practiced these steps, which are important parts of being a great student. And you also don't have to be a student to benefit from these steps. Anyone can do these things. It is vital that we all consider ourselves to be lifelong learners and students, because we should never stop acquiring knowledge. That should be our continual goal to accomplish. We must find ways to use our knowledge to further develop ourselves and our skills. If we don't do this, we will remain stagnant and not move forward. Additionally, our memory will not be as fine-tuned, so we cannot remember what we have learned. But once you have trained yourself to do the different things we have talked about in this chapter, you can be an excellent life student, who will be able to learn just about anything and recall everything. We guarantee that you will see improvement in your overall cognition and ability to take in different kinds of information.

And That's a Wrap

Envision your life is a movie and it is capturing every living moment. Think of a CCTV camera that is on all the time and watching you as you move about every day. That might freak you out, but it also may make you realize that your life is filled with endless moments. We have Kodak moments daily, and we want to always remember them. But often, we get consumed by apps like Instagram, where we love to share pictures of those moments in our lives. You lose yourself in the process of trying to remember something. What we have to do is learn to enjoy our lives and make the memories with our imaginations, using our brains and not the devices that contribute to our daily functions.

This book has demonstrated nine different ways to enhance your photographic memory. First of all, we talked about how to improve your general memory. Focusing on your general memory allows you think of all the ways you create a photographic recollection of the things in your life. This includes things like the Memory Palace, which is a proven way to remember just about anything. Using the Memory Palace will help you spatially locate things in your mind's eye. The second step that we demonstrated was how to use the Military Method to train yourself to remember better. This was a tested method by a Navy SEAL that allowed one man to accomplish the impossible at a memory competition. This is definitely not the only way to do it, but it is something that you can do to workout your mind to do amazing tasks. In the third chapter, we talked about diet and how that impacts your thinking abilities. Diet is one of the most important factors that contributes to our memory's development or decline. By feeding your mind with good food, you can increase your brain's activity and memory retention. On the other hand, unhealthy foods will cause memory decline, leading to disorders, such as Alzheimer's and dementia. We are sure you would like to avoid such cases as far as possible. Chapter 4 dealt with the issue of sleep and how many people don't get the shut-eye they deserve. Sleeping is the time of memory consolidation in which the brain will put together the memories it has assembled throughout the day and puts some of the memories into a permanent storage center. This act allows the brain to retain a lot of information and do all the great things to enhance your life.

In the fifth chapter, we talked about mnemonic devices and how they can get you to remember many things based on the different patterns you form in your mind. For example, you could use acronyms or other helpful hints that train you to recall various concepts. Mnemonic devices are especially helpful when you want to remember dates and other historical facts. Next, in the sixth chapter, we looked at sensory memory and how that enables a person to remember using all the senses. This type of memory is used for actors, who emotionally prepare themselves for roles, where they must empathize and feel the emotions of the character to act out the part on stage or on screen. Although this method is useful for actors, it is also a nifty tool to help you support others who are struggling with their emotions and who are grieving or celebrating their success. In the seventh chapter, we talked about all the ways to cognitively increase your skills. We looked at different exercises that could increase cognitive activity and help you get to where you need to be with your memory. The eighth chapter was about how to make you more mentally alert to handle different challenges, including hydration. You must take these steps to feel at your best every day. Finally, the last chapter dealt with various study hacks that will help you remember all the things you need for tests, presentations, and other tasks you would find at a high school, university, or other academic program.

Putting it all together, we can conclude that creating a photographic memory is not an easy task. It requires a huge investment of your time and resources. You have to give it all you've got, because it's not going to simply come easy to you. There is a reason why it is called memory training, because, like working out at a gym, your mind needs to have activities that will help it to remember the things that continually go on. Our bodies and minds are continually in a state of informational overload. We experience many sensations and emotions every day, which makes us vulnerable to forgetting. Because we are finite beings, there is no way all of that information is getting stored in our brains. Fortunately, to our rescue, we can forget a lot of things, especially the harmful and difficult memories we have. There is a blessing to forgetting, but also it makes it more difficult for us to remember the good times. That is why we rely on cameras, note-taking, and audio recordings to help us to retain the information in one safe place.

If you want to have a photographic memory, you will need to take time to follow the steps we have outlined in this book. Step by step you can get to where you need to be. Memory training is a process, not a destination. It requires your patience, but it also requires spaced repetition. As you are now aware, cramming gets you nowhere, when it comes to permanent memory development. If you want to retain all of those vocabulary words for that test, it takes memorizing a little bit at a time. Additionally, for everything that you study, you must memorize using images. Because our minds are wired for spatial and visual memory, we have to do all that it takes to put the picture in our heads. Otherwise, we will forget. Allow all the sensations of the experience to come to your mind. And then, you will remember better. Don't allow yourself to rely on rote memorization. It never works. Instead, try memorizing information using a variety of techniques that help you to assimilate the data in your head, so you can ace the test or simply remember the everyday experiences that you come across.

Thank you for joining us on this journey. Your personal venture continues for the rest of your life, but we hope that we have been able to guide you through the ways that will lead to your development and personal fulfillment. Take time today to appreciate things in your mind's eye. Turn off your phone or computer, take in the view, and allow your brain to process every experience that you have. Don't rely too much on the technology that is part of your life. Instead, live your life in low-tech, slowed down, and spaced out ways, so that you can live moment to moment with more vigor and excitement than ever before.

Works Cited

Alban, D (2019). 15 Brain Exercises to Keep Your Mind Sharp. [blog] Be Brain Fit. Retrieved from https://bebrainfit.com/brain-exercises/

Boost Your Memory by Eating Right (2012). Harvard Health Publishing: Harvard Medical School. Retrieved from https://www.health.harvard.edu/mind-and-mood/boost-your-memory-by-eating-right

Boureston, K (n.d.) How to Develop a Photographic Memory: The Ultimate Guide. [blog] Mantelligence. Retreived from https://www.mantelligence.com/how-to-develop-a-photographic-memory/

Charlie Brown Christmas: Lucy Van Pelt (n.d.) IMDB. Retrieved from https://www.imdb.com/title/tt0059026/characters/nm0833559

Bergland, C. (2014). Eight Habits that Improve Cognitive Function. Psychology Today. Retrieved from https://www.psychologytoday.com/us/blog/the-athletes-way/201403/eight-habits-improve-cognitive-function

Jennings, K-A (2017). 11 Best Foods to Boost Your Brain and Memory. Healthline. Retrieved from https://www.healthline.com/nutrition/11-brain-foods

Foer, J. (2012). TED Talk: Feats of Memory Anyone Can Do. [Video] Retrieved from https://www.youtube.com/watch?time_continue=905&v=U6PoUg7jXsA

"How Bad is Pulling an All-nighter" (n.d.) Advanced Sleep Medicine Services. Retrieved from https://www.sleepdr.com/the-sleep-blog/how-bad-is-pulling-an-all-nighter/

Kekatos, M (2018). You CAN drink away your troubles, study says: Alcohol affects a gene making your brain forget the bad times and only remember the good ones. Daily Mail Online. Retrieved from https://www.dailymail.co.uk/health/article-6316275/Alcohol-helps-remember-good-times-not-bad-ones-study-says.html

Leyden, A (2019). 20 Study Hacks to Improve Your Memory. Go Conqr. Retrieved from https://www.goconqr.com/en/examtime/blog/study-hacks/

Mnemonic. Merriam Webster Dictionary Online. Retrieved from https://www.merriam-webster.com/dictionary/mnemonic

Noyes, A (1947). The Highwayman. The Poetry Foundation. Retrieved from https://www.poetryfoundation.org/poems/43187/the-highwayman

Psych Central Staff (2018). Memory and Mnemonic Devices. Psych Central. Retrieved from https://psychcentral.com/lib/memory-and-mnemonic-devices/

Robinson, T (2008). "Hannah Montana Cast, "Bones" Dance VERY FUNNY!" [Video] Retrieved from https://www.youtube.com/watch?v=VVwHCDQqRN8

Ron White Memory Expert: Memory Training and Brain Training (2016). How Navy SEAL Mental Training Helped Me Win the USA Memory Championships. [video] Retrieved from https://www.youtube.com/watch?v=6QKUEDBIG6w

Timoney, B (2016). How to Develop Your Sense Memory. Brian Timony Actor's Studio. Retrieved from https://www.briantimoneyacting.co.uk/develop-sense-memory/

Why Do We Sleep, Anyway (n.d.). Healthy Sleep: Harvard Medical School. Retrieved from http://healthysleep.med.harvard.edu/healthy/matters/benefits-of-sleep/why-do-we-sleep

www.ingramcontent.com/pod-product-compliance
Lightning Source LLC
Chambersburg PA
CBHW071355080526
44587CB00017B/3112